Afterthoughts

Afterthoughts

LAWRENCE BLOCK

OPEN ROAD

INTEGRATED MEDIA

NEW YORK

Contents

OTHER PSEUDONYMOUS NOVELS

BOOKS FOR WRITERS

AFTERWORD

Introduction

Sometime in the mid-1990s, I was in residence at Ragdale, a writers colony in Lake Forest, Illinois. I had a six-week stay booked, and upon arrival I went straight to work on what would eventually become *The Burglar in the Library*. I worked hard for perhaps three weeks, and got quite a bit written, but pulled up short when I realized the book had taken a serious wrong turn and I wasn't ready to straighten it out.

Well, these things happen. I had the sense to put the book aside and work on other things. I wrote two stories about Keller that became chapters in *Hit Man*, and I wrote an introduction to a hardcover edition of *The Canceled Czech*. And then, with a week to go, I started work on a memoir.

I hadn't been thinking of this, at least not consciously. But what I decided was that I'd write a book about my early years as a writer, and the words flew out of me. I found I would be writing about something I hadn't thought about in years, and it would lead me to incidents I'd totally forgotten, as various doors in my memory flew open one after another. I worked all day every day, and by the end of the week I'd produced 50,000 words.

Then I went home to New York, where I spent a month surrendering to physical, mental, and emotional exhaustion of a sort I'd never felt before. I had, as best I could figure it, about forty percent of the book written, and my then-agent incorporated that book into a four-book contract with my then-publisher.

A few years later, I bought back the memoir. It was clear to me I was never going to finish it.

I don't know why. Maybe I just wasn't willing to risk that sort of exhaustion again.

I did write a memoir some years later. *Step by Step: A Pedestrian Memoir* began as a record of a year in the life of an aging and unskilled racewalker, and wound up including more material about my early years than I'd anticipated. When I'd finished it I found myself thinking about *A Writer Prepares*. (That's what I'd been calling the earlier memoir, with a nod to Stanislavski's *An Actor Prepares*.) But I didn't even go so far as to read what I'd done earlier.

Then, in 2010, I began writing afterwords to early works I was readying for new lives as ebooks. It seemed to me this would be an easy way to add value to the new editions, and also to put them into perspective for today's reader. Looking back, I suspect there was more to it; I think I wanted to dip into the past, wanted indeed to write autobiographically about my early writing days. And, while I wasn't prepared to resume that memoir from fifteen years earlier, I could cover the same ground incrementally, a book at a time.

And that's what I've done. If I have indeed written a memoir on the installment plan, why shouldn't I put all of those afterwords together into a single volume?

But how to organize the material? When all else fails, I tend

to opt for alphabetical order, but that's no better than other no-
tions that occurred to me. So I've tried to group the books by
type. But these pieces don't have to be read in any particular
sequence. You're certainly free to skip around.

Meanwhile, why shouldn't I add a few other introductions
and afterwords written for other occasions? A few years ago I
wrote introductions for new paperback editions of all eight Evan
Tanner novels, so why not toss them in? The book can find room
for them.

Furthermore, because there's no getting around the fact that
Afterthoughts is likely to lead some readers to sample other books
of mine, I'm able to think of it as a promotional vehicle for all
my works. And this means that I can afford to price it very in-
expensively indeed.

A lot of you have asked for a memoir about my writing
career. This seems to be it. I do hope you enjoy it.

—Lawrence Block
Greenwich Village

Lawrence Block (lawbloc@gmail.com) welcomes your email
responses; he reads them all, and replies when he can.

Lawrence Block Novels

AFTER THE FIRST DEATH

The summer of 1964, I moved from the Buffalo, New York, suburb of Tonawanda to Racine, Wisconsin, to take an editorial position in the coin supply division of Whitman Publishing Company, a division of Western Printing. I enjoyed my time in the corporate world, but a year and a half of it turned out to be enough, and in early 1966 my then-wife and I and our two daughters moved into a large, well-appointed house in New Brunswick, New Jersey. It was down the street from my agent, Henry Morrison, and a block away from Don Westlake, my best friend.

I'd done some non-numismatic (currency-related) writing during my sojourn in Racine, completing the second Jill Emerson novel (*Enough of Sorrow*), a Gold Medal Books crime novel (*The Girl with the Long Green Heart*), and the first Evan Tanner adventure (*The Thief Who Couldn't Sleep*). In New Brunswick I installed my massive oak desk in a third-floor study and went right to work on a second Tanner book. I was freelancing full time again and glad to be back to it.

Once a week I'd go to New York, generally getting a ride in from Henry. I'd participate in a poker game that four or five of us had kicked off in 1960—and that continues to this day, albeit monthly rather than weekly. And sometimes, after the game broke up, I'd pursue other interests in and around Times Square, catching a train home the following afternoon.

Around this time a lot of criminals drew "Get Out of Jail Free" cards, courtesy of some Supreme Court decisions. Because their confessions had been improperly obtained, because they'd been denied counsel, because in one way or another their rights had been violated, they got to walk out and go home—at least until they got picked up for doing the same thing over again.

That was something to think about.

Around the same time, I was having the occasional blackout after the occasional long night of heavy drinking. I didn't get drunk every time I drank, nor did I have a blackout every time I got drunk, but once in a while I'd come to with no recollection of having gone to bed. Sometimes I'd have spotty memories of a couple of hours. Sometimes I'd have no memory at all.

In time I'd learn that blackouts are almost invariably a marker of alcoholism. While not all alcoholics experience them, anyone who does may be said, at the very least, to have something problematic about his drinking. I didn't know that then, and simply regarded blackouts as an unfortunate consequence of having had too much to drink. My blackouts generally consisted of an inability to recall a tedious hour or two at the end of an extended evening, when no one was likely to have said anything worth remembering in the first place. They were, I was fairly certain, something I could learn to avoid.

A fellow I'd worked with a decade ago at the Scott Meredith Literary Agency, a merchant seaman-turned-writer named John

Dobbin, told me how he'd go on a toot on shore leave and wake up a couple of days later. In Cuba, he said, he came to in a bed with six prostitutes. I sort of envied him. Hey, nothing like that had ever happened to me.

Suppose a man woke up in a Times Square hotel with a splitting headache and no recollection of going there. Suppose he wasn't alone. Suppose there was a woman there, one he'd never seen before.

Suppose she was dead.

Suppose this had happened before. Suppose he went to jail for it, and a Supreme Court decision got him through the revolving door and back on the street.

Suppose he did it again.

Well, there was the premise. I wrote the first chapter of what would turn out to be *After the First Death* and showed it to Don Westlake. "There's one thing you don't have to worry about," he told me. "Nobody who reads this chapter will be able to keep from going on to the next one."

After the First Death was unquestionably the most personal book I'd written. The pseudonymous soft-core erotic novels were, for the most part, derivative fantasies; the lesbian fiction, however earnest and well-intentioned, was the projection of some sort of alter ego. The various crime novels and, certainly, the Tanner books had characters with whom I could identify— but they weren't me, and their life experiences were not mine.

This book came closer. The blackouts, the hookers—there was a lot of my life that found its way into Alex Penn's life. He was not me nor I him, but we had a few things in common.

And his girlfriend, I should say, was drawn from life. Her long speech, about an affair that didn't work out, is pretty close to verbatim.

Macmillan published the book. It was my second hardcover, appearing two years after *Deadly Honeymoon*. It didn't set the world on fire, but then I never expected to touch off a global conflagration. It's been in and out of print over the years, and I'm pleased to have it available now in ebook form.

Quite a few years passed and a great many books written before I wrote again about drinking and blackouts. *The Sins of the Fathers* came out in 1976, and was the first of seventeen novels about one Matthew Scudder. Some people see *After the First Death* as a precursor to the Scudder books, and there's certainly a thematic connection. And again to state what should be obvious: I'm not Matthew Scudder, and he's not me. But we have a few things in common.

ARIEL

In 1995, G & G Books, a creature of Ed Gorman and Marty Greenberg, had a project in the works that they called The Lawrence Block Library. Their first entry was a first hardcover edition of the third Matthew Scudder book, *In the Midst of Death*. It sold out right away, so they followed it with *Ariel*. I tried to steer them in another direction, because *Ariel* had already been published in hardcover by Arbor House, and it seemed to me that collector demand for a second hardcover edition would be minimal. Indeed it was, and the book did not sell well. That, alas, was the end of The Lawrence Block Library, but the book did include an author's afterword and here it is:

In the summer of 1975 my life was in what one of Sean O'Casey's characters would call a state of chassis. A thirteen-year marriage had ended two years previously, and my totem ever since seemed to be that legendary bird born with one wing shorter than the other, and consequently doomed to fly around in ever-diminishing concentric circles.

Each of my relationships ended a little more quickly than the one before it. This pattern reached full bloom in July, when I cleaned out my apartment on West Fifty-eighth Street, Manhattan, sold or gave away almost everything I had left after the divorce, and crammed everything that remained into a Ford station wagon that was in no better shape than I was. I drove to Buffalo, where I was to move in with a blameless young woman with whom I'd been keeping company.

When I pulled into her driveway, she came out to meet me, a mask of concern on her face. "I don't think this is going to work," she said.

"Now you tell me," I said.

I thought about that bird, the one with wings of unequal length, the one flying in ever-diminishing concentric circles. Such birds are rare, and for good reason. What happens to the bird, ultimately, is that he flies up his own asshole and disappears.

And that, in a manner of speaking, is what I decided to do. I sorted the stuff in the Ford wagon, gave about half of it away, and stowed the rest in my mother's attic. Then, after spending a reasonably carefree month on Fire Island, New York, with my daughters, I got back into the Ford and pointed it south.

I had a sort of a plan. Since I didn't seem capable of living anyplace, I was going to try living no place. I was on my way to California, but I was in no hurry to get there. In the meantime, I would try to operate with two ground rules. I would not stay anywhere for more than a month, and I would try to get out of town before I was asked to.

Along the way, I'd do what I always did. I'd support myself by writing.

This was what I'd always done, although I seemed less deft at it lately. Since the marriage broke up I'd written the fourth Chip Harrison book and the first three Matthew Scudder novels, along with what would turn out to be the last of many pseudonymous works. But that was all in the first fifteen months or so, and now it had been almost a year since I'd managed to get anything finished. I was starting to get a little nervous, sort of like a Christian Scientist with appendicitis, but at least I knew what I was going to do next, because my agent had landed me a contract. I was going to write a book called *The Adopted*, about an adoption that didn't work out.

Not my idea. It was the prospective publisher's idea, and I pretended to know what he had in mind. Then I went off and pretended to write it.

First place I went was Rodanthe, on North Carolina's Outer Banks. I spent a month there, fishing off the long pier, literally existing on what I hauled out of the water. I wrote a couple of short stories, but what I mostly did was fish.

I drove from there to Greenville, South Carolina, where I knew an advertising executive from New York and an Irish songwriter from Listowel, County Kerry. They didn't know each other, but both of them happened to know a woman who'd recently split with her husband,

and one of them arranged for me to take her to dinner. We went out and had a nice time, and she seemed to like me and I seemed to like her, so when I woke up the next day I threw all my stuff in the car and drove to Charleston.

In Charleston I got a room at Rooms. That's all the sign said, so I always assumed that was the name of the place. Staying at a place called Rooms, I can assure you, ranks right up there with eating at a place called Mom's and playing cards with a man named Doc. Don't ever do it.

My room cost twenty dollars a week. That's not much money nowadays, and it wasn't much money twenty years ago, either, yet no one could have claimed the place was underpriced. Rooms was on Fulton Street in downtown Charleston, and I looked for it when I returned to Charleston some six or seven years later for a visit. Now Charleston, as you may know, is the preservationist capital of America. You pitch a tent in the park, someone'll stop you when you try to take it down. In Charleston, BHT's the drug of choice. They preserve everything.

They may be crazy, but they're not stupid. They tore down Rooms.

But not while I was there. I set up my typewriter and tried to write *The Adopted*. I didn't seem to be getting anywhere, though. I went to a Unitarian breakfast and met a woman and had a couple of dates with her, and I called the one in Greenville and she came down for the weekend. Then I got in the car and was on my way again. I spent a week or so on Jekyll Island, Georgia. I remember there was a restaurant that had an all-you-can-eat special on boiled shrimp, and I remember there was a lunar eclipse, and that's about all I remember. I got back in the car and drove to St. Augustine, Florida, and holed up in a motel. I stayed drunk for a couple of days, and then I drank a bottle of cough syrup, and then I went to work and wrote *Ariel*, which is what *The Adopted* turned out to want to call itself. "I am Ariel, the Adopted," I typed, and I just stayed with it until it was done. It took a few weeks.

I know I was done by Christmas, because I remember taking the manuscript with me to Greenville. (I flew there to spend the holiday with the lady. She read it and said she liked it, but she liked me, too, so what does that say about her judgment?) I mailed the manuscript to my agent and flew back to Jacksonville, where I'd left my car. My daughters flew down to spend a week of vacation with me, and then they went back to New York and I went to Naples, Florida. The car broke down. I got it fixed and drove to Destin, Florida, and Mobile, Alabama. In Mobile I tried to write a fourth book about Matthew Scudder, but after thirty or forty pages I tore it up and got in the car again. I drove to Sardis, Mississippi.

On and on and on.

In Roswell, New Mexico, I realized that all over America there were men who got up every morning, put on suits and went off to offices. I wondered how the hell they did it. I'd tried to get a job in Charleston, while I was living at Rooms. There was a shoe repairman around the corner who had a sign in his window, Apprentice Wanted. I was thirty-seven years old, I'd been writing professionally for almost twenty years, and I went in and applied for the job.

"Here's the situation," he said. "I'll spend a lot of time training someone, and then just when he starts to earn his keep, he'll leave. So the one thing I want to know is will you stay?"

I just couldn't lie to the man. I told him I didn't expect to hang around Charleston all that long.

"Well, I appreciate your honesty," he said, "but I have to say I'm sorry to hear that. Because I'm a pretty good judge of people, and I'd say you've got the makings of a damn good shoemaker."

I thought about this in Roswell. That was my chance, I thought, and I went and blew it.

Meanwhile, I heard nothing about *Ariel*. I couldn't get anything out of my agent, who swore he couldn't get anything out of the publisher. I finally got to L.A., and I finally got back from L.A. and wound up in New York again. By then it was the end of '76 and I'd written the first Bernie Rhodenbarr novel and Random House was set to publish it. By then, too, the other publisher had said no to *Ariel*. My agent tried it a couple of places and it didn't stick anywhere.

Let's fast-forward a couple of years. I was living on Greenwich Street, still in New York, and I had a new agent, and I dug out *Ariel* and showed it to him. He sent it to Donald I. Fine at Arbor House, who wanted to do it if I'd rewrite it. I looked at it and agreed it was a mess and started over from the beginning. I enlarged the original version by a third or so, and I made the setting specifically Charleston. (That's what it was in the first version, but I hadn't come right out and said so.)

Don Fine loved the finished version, and published it with muted fanfare in 1980. For several years after that he asked me when I was going to write another book like *Ariel*. I don't know, I said.

Never, I could have said.

What's remarkable, it seems to me, isn't that I never wrote another book like *Ariel* but that I wrote the thing at all. It's entirely unlike anything else I've done before or since. What I liked most about it was writing the scenes with Ariel and Erskine. The two of them were very vivid in my mind, and remain so. I'm not as taken with other elements of the book, including the ending. I'd have ended the book differently if I could have figured out how. Some people were bothered by the ending, finding it ambiguous, and other people liked the ending *because* of its ambiguity.

Make what you will of that. (Lawrence Block, "Afterword," *Ariel*, G & G Books, 1996)

I was happy to see *Ariel* back in print, and in such a handsome edition. The book had been out of print since Berkley Books' paperback edition came and went. (They paid a healthy advance for the book, but the cover was hideous and they didn't sell many copies. The Arbor House edition didn't sell many copies, either, but at least it had an attractive cover.) But, as I said, the book didn't sell in its Lawrence Block Library edition, and I'm glad it has a new life as an ebook.

Enough. If you've read *Ariel*, you don't really need me to tell you what you just read. And if you *haven't* read the book, if you actually skipped ahead and read the afterword first, well, you're probably the sort of person who first swallows the antacid and then eats the chili.

And who the hell am I to criticize you for it?

CINDERELLA SIMS

Look, this wasn't my idea.

Three or four years ago, Bill Schafer of Subterranean Press suggested that I might give some consideration to republishing a book of mine called *$20 Lust*, which had originally appeared under the name Andrew Shaw. I recalled the book he meant but dimly; I had, after all, written it in 1960. But I didn't need to remember it all that vividly to know the answer to his suggestion.

"No," I told him.

A little later I suggested he might want to publish a fancy edition of *Grifter's Game*, the first book under my own name; it had come out as a paperback original, then called *Mona*, in 1961, and we could celebrate its fortieth anniversary with a nice limited edition hardcover.

Bill was lukewarm to the notion but had an alternative proposal; how about issuing a double volume containing *Grifter's Game* and *$20 Lust*? Once again, I didn't have to do a lot of soul-searching to come up with a response.

"No," I told him.

Time passed. Then Ed Gorman, the Sage of Cedar Rapids, reprinted an ancient private eye novelette of mine in a pulp anthology. When it came out he sent me a copy, and although I didn't read my novelette—I figured it was enough that I wrote the damned thing—I did read his introduction, which I found to be thoughtful, incisive, and generous. I emailed him and told him so, and he emailed me back and thanked me, adding that my early work was probably better than I thought.

"And," he added, "I really think you ought to consider letting Bill Schafer publish *$20 Lust.*"

I felt as though I'd been sucker punched. Where the hell did that come from?

So I got in touch with Bill. "I suppose I could at least read it," I said, "except I can't, because I don't have a copy." He did, or maybe he got one from Ed; in either case, a battered copy arrived in the mail. I looked at the first two pages and I looked at the last two or three pages, and I heaved a sigh. Heaved it clear across the room and would have heaved the book, too, but instead I hollered for my wife, Lynne.

"Bill Schafer wants to reprint this," I said.

"Great," she said.

"Not necessarily," I said, and explained the circumstances. "I'd like you to read this," I said, "or as much of it as you can without gagging, and then tell me it's utter crap and I'd surely destroy what little reputation I have if I consent to its republication."

"Suppose I like it?"

"Not to worry," I said. "I'll sign the commitment papers, and I'll make sure they take real good care of you."

She found herself a comfortable chair and got to work.

While she's reading, I'll tell you what I remember about the book.

In the spring of 1960, I got married. My future ex-wife and I took an apartment on West Sixty-ninth Street between Columbus and Amsterdam Avenues. I installed a desk in our bedroom and planted a typewriter on top of it. I was writing a book a month for a publisher of what we'd now call soft-core porn, but which we then knew as sex novels. Veiled descriptions, no naughty words—but, within those limitations, as arousing as possible. Books, in short, to be read with one hand.

I was doing other things as well, trying to write better books and stories for more respectable markets.

Sometimes a book would start out in one direction and wind up changing course. *Grifter's Game*, of which I spoke earlier, is a case in point. After I wrote the first chapter, it occurred to me that this might have possibilities. I stayed with it and wrote it as well as I could, and Henry Morrison, then my agent, agreed that it was a cut above the other stuff, and sent it to Gold Medal Books, where Knox Burger bought it.

Similarly, my second book started out as a TV tie-in novel, a thousand-dollar quickie based on *Markham*, a short-lived detective series starring Ray Milland. I was pleased with the way it turned out and so was Henry and Knox; I changed the character's name from Roy Markham to Ed London, and called the book *Coward's Kiss*. (Gold Medal called it *Death Pulls a Doublecross*. In recent years its original title has been restored.)

Now where does *$20 Lust* fit into this scheme of things? Good question, and I'm not sure I can answer it. Ed Gorman sees it as a precursor to *Grifter's Game*, but I'm not sure that's the case; it may as easily have been written after *Grifter's Game*.

What I do know is that it represents a reversal of the earlier pattern, in which I'd started out to write a sow's ear and wound up with, well, call it a polyester handbag. I set out with the intention of writing a Gold Medal–type crime novel, and somewhere along the way I decided it wasn't good enough and finished it up as a sex novel. I don't remember when this happened, only that I was still at that desk and in that apartment at the time. (I was there for nine months, until the end of the year, when my ex-to-be and I moved to 444 Central Park West. We took the desk along, and indeed took it to Tonawanda, New York; to Racine, Wisconsin; and to New Brunswick, New Jersey, where I had to cut off two of its feet to get it upstairs to my third-floor office at 16 Stratford Place. There, for all I know, it remains to this day.)

I called the finished book *Cinderella Sims.* My publisher called it *$20 Lust.* And poor Lynne wound up stuck with the chore of reading it. Well, better she than I.

"It's not that bad," she said. My heart sank.

"It's not," she said, just in case I hadn't heard her the first time. "It's not Shakespeare, but I don't think it'll do you any harm to publish it."

"Oh," I said.

"It's politically incorrect," she pointed out. "Sexist, racist, homophobic, at least in today's terms. But so's everything else written that long ago."

"Not to mention Shakespeare," I pointed out.

"Who mentioned Shakespeare?"

"You did."

"Oh," she said. "I did? I wonder why. Anyway, I think you should read it."

"Do I have to?"

She gave me a look, and she gave me the book, and I didn't exactly read it because reading very early work of mine makes me sick to my stomach. But I skimmed enough of it to realize that it was a far cry from pornographic and really didn't have much sexual content at all. I'd evidently gotten fairly far with it before I gave up on it and finished it for the sex novel house.

I wonder what made me do that.

Hell, who knows? Who knows why the kid that I was did any of the things he did?

What I had to decide was whether to republish the book. I weighed various considerations, and was reminded of Mae West's observation. When she had to choose one of two evils, she said, she made it a point to pick the one she hadn't tried yet. Similarly, when I have to pick a course of action, I tend to choose the one that brings money into our house. And, while I don't suppose *Cinderella Sims* will wrap Lynne in sable, it should provide a few coins for that polyester handbag.

So there you are. Subterranean Press turned out a fine-looking, well-made volume, and it's now my pleasure to see it reissued as an ebook.

AN APPRECIATION BY ED GORMAN

I wrote the following as a way of setting up a Larry Block novelette I was reprinting in an anthology of pulp stories. I don't see any reason to change a word. Not because they're such graceful or pithy words but because they convey my feelings about Lawrence Block the writer.

Lawrence Block writes the best sentences in the business, that business being crime fiction. No tortured self-conscious arty stuff, either. Just pure, graceful, skilled writing of a very high order.

No matter what he writes—the dark Scudder private eye novels; the spunky Bernie Rhodenbarrs about the kind of thief even a mom could love; or his latest creation, John Keller the hitman, an existential figure full of quirks and kindnesses rare in his profession—no matter what he's telling us, he always makes it sweet to read. He's just so damned nimble and graceful and acute with his language.

By now, his story is pretty well known. Wrote a lot of erotica in the late fifties and early sixties, all the while writing his early crime paperback originals and stories for magazines of every kind. Started becoming a name in crime fiction in the seventies, really broke out in the nineties and is now posed, one would think, for superstardom.

Block has always reminded me of a very intelligent fighter. He knows what he's good at and sticks to his own fight, unmoved by popular fads and critical fancies. He writes about women as well as any male writer I've ever read (though since I'm a guy, I may just be saying that he perceives women the same way I do) and he deals with subjects as Oprah-ready as alcoholism and failed fatherhood realistically yet without resorting to weepiness.

One senses in him sometimes a frustrated mainstream writer. He's always pushing against the restrictions of form and yet never failing to give the reader what he came for in the first place. No easy trick, believe me.

For some reason, I've always hated the word *wordsmith* (probably because it's popular among pretentious young advertising copywriters who don't want to admit that they're writing hymns to beer and dish soap), but that's what Block is. A singer of songs, a teller of tales, a bedazzler.

I read three of his erotic novels, and I'll tell you something. They're better written (and we're talking 1958–61) than half the contemporary novels I read today. He was pushing against form even back then, creating real people and real problems, and doing so in a simple, powerful voice that stays with you a hell of a long time.

I always say that I'm glad to see writers make it up from the trenches and into the sunshine of national prominence. Few writers spent so long in the trenches. Larry sold his first story in 1958. He first hit big in the middle 1990s. That's a long time to breathe the dusty, sometimes dank air of literary obscurity.

Larry began his career, as most of us know by now, selling short stories to the crime magazines of the time and to the sort of paperbacks that local religious groups were always trying to drive from the newsstands. The motley crew of outcasts I hung with in my early college years called these books, as I recall, right-handers—suggesting that this type of book inspired one to a certain kind of action few other books did. Except maybe for *Peyton Place* and its imitators. The underlined passages.

In those days I read a lot of novels published by Midwood Tower and Beacon Books and Nightstand Books. I quickly came to realize that some of the writers were much better than others. Max Collier, for example, wrote some of the most perverse books I've ever read. As I remember them, he frequently paired up his bitter hunchbacked heroes with heiresses. Clyde Allison was usually thin on plot but great with patter. Orrie Hitt sometimes got too perverse for my tastes but usually supplied a kind of second-rate James T. Farrell–like blue collar take on the standard "sexy" plots.

And when I say *sexy*, I mean sexy in the way of the movie

comedies of the 1950s and early 1960s. Short on actual details but long on suggestion. And metaphor. Orgasms were frequently portrayed as "searing volcanoes" or some such.

A few of the right-handers were written reasonably well. No great masterpieces slipped through, you understand, but some of the books were actually . . . kinda, sorta actual novels rather than just the usual monthly tease.

Which brings us to some guy named Andrew Shaw.

This was one of Larry Block's pen names circa 1959–61. Other writers would share the name later on (someday somebody will do an article on how contracts secretly get handed off from writer to writer, a particular form of "ghosting" that goes on at the lower levels of publishing even today), but the early Shaws, at least those I've read, read like Larry Block.

Not the Larry Block of today. The Shaw prose isn't especially polished; the Shaw stories don't always escape cliché; and the Shaw attitude is not unlike the hard-boiled crime fiction magazines of the day—i.e., too tough for its own good.

And yet.

Yet you can see in glimpses—and sometimes sustained for long stretches—the Larry Block of today. The idiosyncratic take on modern morality; the dour irony that hides fear and loneliness; and the seeds—just planted—of the style that would become the best of his generation.

Cinderella Sims was originally published as *$20 Lust*. The editor obviously spent a long time coming up with that one.

I'm not sure what else Larry was writing at that time. I suspect he was upgrading for an assault on Gold Medal and better paying markets. I say this because *Cinderella Sims* seems to fall between his sexy books and his early Gold Medal books. Not quite worthy of that little gold medallion but damned close.

One thing Larry Block always had was the ability to move a story forward while giving you detailed character sketches. He has a fast eye for the unusual, the quirks in us, and he makes us come alive with these details. That skill is already apparent in the novel you're holding. And so is his skill in giving you journalistic snapshots of urban America. Rereading *Cinderella Sims* today is like traveling back in time to that pre-hippie sixties when crew cuts were still the style on college campuses and free love was something only the ridiculous Hugh Hefner experienced.

I'm not going to tell you that this is a great book because it isn't. But it's a damned interesting look at the artist-in-making. I think you'll agree with me, that from the very beginning of his career, Larry Block was a vital and powerful storyteller.

COWARD'S KISS

Early in my writing career, I was a curious sort of marksman. The only way I could hit a target was by aiming below it.

The first book published under my name was a Gold Medal Books crime novel, *Grifter's Game*. (*Mona* was the title a publisher hung on it, to fit a piece of mediocre cover art he had on hand; it's original title has since been restored.) The manuscript started out to be a soft-core erotic novel, but a few chapters in I got more ambitious for it, and my agent sent it to Fawcett, where it landed.

I tried to come up with an idea for a second book for Gold Medal, but couldn't. This had to do, I'm sure, with murky issues of self-esteem, and if this were a therapy session we could delve into them more deeply—but it's not, so the hell with it.

Then my agent came along with an assignment, and I agreed

to write a tie-in novel for a paperback publisher called Belmont. Belmont Books is long gone—and no great loss, I shouldn't think—but TV tie-ins still exist, and my friend Lee Goldberg does some excellent ones based on *Monk*. The idea, then as now, was that fans of a popular series would want to read new adventures of their favorite characters, which the novelist would spin out to 60,000 words or so.

Belmont wanted a tie-in novel based on *Markham,* a private eye series starring Ray Milland that ran for the 1959–60 season. It seemed to me Roy Markham smoked a pipe, and I'm pretty sure he drove a Renault Dauphine, a choice he made in deference to the show's sponsor. Now that I think about it, I may have made up the pipe. The Renault, I assure you, was not my idea.

So I wrote the book, and it turned out pretty well. By the time I got to the end of it I decided it was too good to be a one thousand dollar tie-in novel, and my agent agreed and sent it to Knox Burger at Gold Medal Books, who'd bought and published *Grifter's Game.* Knox liked it enough to buy it, and we decided to work out a new name for the lead character.

I thought London would be a good surname for him, perhaps as a nod to Ray Milland's background, and Knox thought London was probably OK. I said Roy seemed all right, and Knox said the name Roy sounded to him like all the shit-kicking hillbilly sergeants who gave him a hard time in basic training. Oh, I said. How about Ed? He said Ed was OK.

He had a plot point or two as well, and I went home—I was living on West Sixty-ninth Street at the time—and tweaked the book enough to make everybody happy. I called it *Coward's Kiss.* When it came out it bore the title *Death Pulls a Doublecross.* You call that a title? Phooey, I say.

So I'd sold twice to Gold Medal by aiming at lower markets. My second book was about a private eye, and if a private eye can be in one book he can be in a dozen, can't he? Anthony Boucher (yes, *the* Anthony Boucher) gave *Death Pulls a Doublecross* a decent review in the *New York Times Book Review*. (Yes, *the* NYTBR.) Not a screaming rave, but an OK review. So the next thing to do was write another book about Ed London, right?

I never did.

You know, I just now learned that Ray Milland wasn't English after all. He was Welsh, born in the town of Neath. If I'd known that, Ed London might have been Ed Cardiff instead. Do you suppose that would have made it easier for me to write a second book?

Probably not.

God knows I tried. I wrote a few chapters of something I was going to call *Dusty Death*, but nothing happened. I made another attempt. And on three occasions I wrote magazine novelettes starring Ed London, published in one of the man's magazines. Not of the *Playboy* ilk, but *Argosy* or *True* magazine wannabes. Those novelettes got collected just a few years ago as *The Lost Cases of Ed London*, published by the small press of Crippen & Landru, and were later folded into the HarperCollins volume, *One Night Stands and Lost Weekends*.

But before I wrote the novelettes, before I wrote anything else, I had to write that book for Belmont.

But that's another story, and you can read about it in the afterword for the book in question, *You Could Call It Murder*. Meanwhile, I hope you enjoyed *Coward's Kiss*, but not so much that you'll be disappointed if I never write a sequel.

* * *

DEADLY HONEYMOON

It wasn't my idea.

The premise of *Deadly Honeymoon,* that is. It was my friend Don Westlake's idea, and I remember the evening he recounted it to me. My then-wife and I were at an upper flat in Brooklyn's remote Canarsie neighborhood, where Don and his then-wife lived. We'd get together a few times a month, at their place or ours, and sit for hours talking and listening to records. And, as often as not, drinking something.

Don and I sometimes showed each other work in progress on evenings like that. I remember reading a dozen pages he'd typed on the same model Smith Corona manual portable typewriter that he'd use for the next half century. In those pages a man was striding purposefully across the George Washington Bridge when a motorist offers him a lift; the fellow—Parker, by name—told him to go to hell.

"This is great," I said, or words to that effect. Do you know where it's going?"

"No," he said, "but I think it'll be interesting to find out."

Indeed. Don wrote twenty-four books about Parker without ever telling us his first name; the last, *Dirty Money,* was published in 2008 a few months before Don's death.

Besides showing each other what we'd been writing, Don and I talked about what we were thinking of writing, and one night Don mentioned an idea he had: a young couple on their honeymoon, the groom beaten up and the bride raped, and the couple, rather than report the incident to the police, decide to seek justice on their own. Did he have a title? He did. *Deadly Honeymoon.*

We drank some more beer and talked of other things, and

that was that. This would have been in 1961. By the middle of the following year my wife and infant daughter and I had relocated to a house in a suburb of Buffalo, New York, and Don and his wife and sons had moved to a house in Englishtown, New Jersey. And it would have been sometime in 1963–4 that I picked up the phone and called him.

"Remember *Deadly Honeymoon*? Did you ever do anything with that idea?" He hadn't. "Well, do you think you're going to?" He allowed that it seemed unlikely. "Here's the thing," I said. "I can't get it out of my head. Would you mind if I took a crack at it?"

He told me to go ahead.

So I did.

I don't remember much about the actual writing of *Deadly Honeymoon*, which suggests that it went smoothly enough. It was published in 1967 by Macmillan, and constituted my first appearance in hardcover. Everyone assumed this was a Big Step Up for me, and in a way I suppose it was, but I knew the book had not gone to Macmillan until half a dozen paperback publishers, starting with the folks at Gold Medal Books who'd brought out *Mona* (now *Grifter's Game*) and *Death Pulls a Doublecross* (now *Coward's Kiss*) had declined to publish it. Gold Medal had paid a two thousand five hundred dollar advance for each of the books they'd done, while Macmillan was willing to go a thousand dollars.

Still, hardcover publishers took you to lunch, and I got two or three very pleasant lunches with my editor, a thoroughly charming woman named Mary Heathcote. That has to count for something. And my parents were very proud, and that's something, too.

When Don read the book, his reaction was interesting. He liked my idea of having Dave and Jill go after the bad guys together. "I'd have sent her home to her parents for the duration," he said, "or stuck her in a motel somewhere. And he'd have done it all on his own, and then reclaimed his bride in triumph."

Here's the thing—I'd always assumed, from that initial moment in Canarsie, that their revenge would be a team effort. That was the idea I thought I was stealing. But it turned out that I'd stolen that part of the idea from my own self.

Never mind. I dedicated the book to Don. Least I could do.

It was my agent Henry Morrison who sold *Deadly Honeymoon* to Macmillan, and the ink was barely dry on the book's first printing when he sold movie rights to producer William Castle. No end of screenwriters took a shot at adapting it, and the project just got worse and worse as it went long. The film did get made and was released rather tentatively in 1973 with the title *Nightmare Honeymoon*. It starred Dack Rambo and Rebecca Dianna Smith, with Pat Hingle as the crime boss, and it was set in New Orleans. And, let us come right out and say it, it stank on ice.

In case you were wondering, it's not available from Netflix. And that's okay with me.

In book form, *Deadly Honeymoon* has been in and out of print over the years. Macmillan sold paperback rights to Dell Publishing, and a couple of other paperback houses have reprinted it since then. And now it's available as an ebook, and isn't that a wonder?

A DIET OF TREACLE

In the summer of 1956, after a freshman year at Antioch College, I came to New York to spend three months in the mail room at Pines Publications. I'd be rooming with Paul Grillo, who'd arrived a few days before me and found us a place to live, at 147 West Fourteenth Street. We were there for two weeks and then found a less expensive place to stay at 108 West Twelfth. By then we'd acquired another roommate, Fred Anliot, and the three of us were sharing a squalid little cell that a solitary midget would have found confining. Two weeks of that and we moved again, to a first-floor apartment at 54 Barrow Street, where we remained until our three months was up and it was time to return to campus.

The job was supposed to provide valuable vocational experience, and I'm sure it did. The guy who ran the promotion and publicity department took me aside one day and said his assistant was leaving and would I like to replace him? I was all set to go for it, and said maybe I'd drop out of school—and that led him to rescind the offer. If I was a student, he said, I should stay in school. That would be more valuable to me than the job he was offering.

I'm not sure he was right about that. The real education was being on my own and living in the Village and meeting all sorts of fascinating folk. I still know some of the people I met on Sunday afternoons around the fountain in Washington Square. A few of them are gone, and I miss them, even as I miss those days and nights.

A few years later I wrote a book set in that time and place. I called it *A Diet of Treacle*, with an epigraph quote from *Alice in Wonderland*. It wound up at Beacon Books, where they published it with the title *Pads Are for Passion*. I used a pen name on the book— Sheldon Lord, a name I'd used before and would use again.

Years passed, as they're apt to do. Hard Case Crime, which had reprinted several of my early crime novels, was casting about for something else of mine, and I remembered the book. Founder Charles Ardai not only liked the book, he even liked its original title.

And, wonder of wonders, *Publishers Weekly* had these nice things to say about this early effort:

Block's New York is a noir wonderland, populated with junkies and beatsters (the dark predecessor to the modern hipster) spouting angular tough-guy dialogue . . . Block effortlessly immerses himself in . . . their world of drugs, sex, and disaffection with a matter-of-factness that hits hard, all the more convincing because Block never makes an overt effort to convince. A potboiler morality play at its finest. ("Fiction Reviews," *Publishers Weekly*, October 2007)

Well, that's generous of them, innit? Possibly more generous than this very early work deserves, but that's OK. I'll take it, and I'm glad to see it go on to a further existence as an ebook. I hope you've enjoyed it.

And as for its author, I've moved around a bit since that first sojourn in the Village. I've lived at various times in upstate New York, in New Jersey, in Wisconsin, in California and Florida; within New York City I've had apartments on the Upper West Side, in Washington Heights, and in Brooklyn's Greenpoint. But I've spent most of my time where I started, in Greenwich Village, and for the past twenty years I've lived within a half mile of that first place on West Fourteenth Street. Sometimes it seems as though I've come a long way. Other times I don't seem to have gone very far at all.

THE GIRL WITH THE LONG GREEN HEART

I can't really improve on this Amazon.com review by Craig Clarke:

"I love a good long-con tale, and *The Girl with the Long Green Heart* is one of the best. Block devises a con so well, it makes you wonder if he hasn't been involved in a little "research" himself. Written in the first person, *The Girl with the Long Green Heart* has a lot of internal monologue from John's point of view. Much of it has to do with the planning of the job, but a preponderance is simply one man's thoughts when thrust into a set of situations he did not plan on, and Block manages to somehow make it all utterly riveting. (Craig Clarke, "Another Great HCC Title from Block," review of *The Girl with the Long Green Heart*, by Lawrence Block, Amazon.com, November 17, 2005)

The review likens the book to *The Sting*, the 1973 film starring Paul Newman and Robert Redford, with Robert Shaw as the perfect bad guy/fall guy. The comparison strikes me as reasonable, but every once in a while some genius decides I ripped off *The Sting*. Since my book was published half a dozen years before the film came out, well, I don't think so. Nor do I feel ill-used by the filmmakers; I'd say both their film and my book owed a bit to David Maurer's nonfiction work *The Big Con*.

There's been occasional film and TV interest in *The Girl with the Long Green Heart*, but nothing's ever come of it. A producer bought me lunch once, and I went home to wait for a check and a contract and a deal to write a pilot—but lunch was as far as that deal got, and that's farther than these things generally get. I once coauthored a book called *Swiss Shooting Talers and Medals*, and the only reason I mention it is that nobody ever seems to have considered adapting it for the screen. I'll tell you, that really sets it apart.

I read *The Girl with the Long Green Heart* again to prepare it for ebook publication, and did so just days after doing the same with *Grifter's Game*. What struck me was how much

I'd developed as a writer in the four or five years between the writing of the two books. I'd like to think I've learned a thing or two since *Long Green Heart*, but I have to say it has nothing to apologize for.

I was living in Tonawanda, a suburb of Buffalo, when I began the book, and I went to Toronto, Canada, and Olean, New York, to research the scenes I set there. (Years later a professor at Olean's St. Bonaventure University booked me for a talk and reading; the book was a hot ticket in Olean, let me tell you, if nowhere else in the known universe.)

Halfway through the writing, I moved to Racine, Wisconsin, to take a job with a numismatic (currency) magazine, and I finished the book in Racine, getting up early to put in a couple of hours before I went to the office. Gold Medal Books was the first publishing house to see the book, and they took it.

As you might guess from the book's ending, I had it in mind that John Hayden and Doug Rance might team up again sometime, and that I might chronicle their subsequent adventures. It never happened, and I can't recall ever giving it much thought. I'm pleased, though, that their sole caper has survived them by almost a half century, and I can but hope that you've enjoyed it.

GRIFTER'S GAME

This turned out to be the first book published under my own name, although I assumed it would be pseudonymous soft-core porn when I started it. A couple of chapters in I decided that this book might be a cut above what I'd been writing, so I wrote it as a crime novel with the hope it might work for Gold

Medal Books. They were the first house to see it, and Knox Burger bought it. I can't recall that he asked for any changes.

But they changed the title. I'd called it *The Girl on the Beach*, because that was such a Charles Williams / Gil Brewer / Peter Rabe title, perfect for Gold Medal. Knox didn't like it. Go figure. Then somebody, he or I or my agent, came up with *Grifter's Game*, and that was one everybody liked.

Next thing I knew, it was published as *Mona*. Years later I learned from Knox that this was publisher Ralph Daigh's idea. He'd bought a painting of a woman's face from an illustrator and wanted a chance to use it on something. If he'd used a portrait of himself, I might be the author of *Horse's Ass*.

The book has had various titles over the years. Someone used the phrase "sweet slow death" in a cover blurb, and Berkley made *that* the title on their reprint edition. When Hard Case Crime brought out the book a couple of years ago, we finally got to call it *Grifter's Game*.

Going over the story prior to ebook publication, I found it remarkable how many of the book's fifty thousand words seem to be devoted to the lighting, smoking, and stubbing out of cigarettes. I'm surprised lung cancer didn't take Joe Marlin out of the picture before the plot had run its course. I noticed, too, that I always used the word "lighted." As in "I lighted a cigarette." Do people talk that way? I never did, so why should Joe Marlin? I changed all those instances of *lighted* to *lit*. And I couldn't resist the chance to fix the occasional infelicitous phrase here and there.

But I didn't do much to it. The book was written in 1960 in a small apartment on West Sixty-ninth Street between Columbus and Amsterdam Avenues. I'd moved to 444 Central Park West by the time it came out in 1961. The fact that it's still around strikes me as remarkable, but then

I'm still around, too, and that's no less remarkable. Here's to both of us!

KILLING CASTRO

In February or March of 1961 my then-wife and I were living in a spacious apartment in a luxury building with Central Park across the street and a slum on our other three sides. She was more than slightly pregnant, and I was too young to worry much about the upcoming obligations of fatherhood. I was writing, and selling what I wrote, and there was nothing wrong with that.

One day my agent, Henry Morrison, came to me with an assignment. Charles Heckelmann, an editor at Monarch Books, itself a second-rate paperback house, had a book he wanted written. The title was to be *Fidel Castro Assassinated*, and that pretty much tells you what he had in mind, but that didn't keep him from spelling it out. "A group of Americans go to Cuba," he said, "and their mission is to assassinate Castro, and they do. They pull it off."

Now he might have gotten the idea from *The Day of the Jackal*, but that would have required more in the way of precognition than Charlie could bring to the table, as Frederick Forsyth's novel wouldn't appear for another ten years. Matter of fact, I believe I know where he got the idea, and the question of precognition, or more specifically the lack thereof, is very much a part of it.

He got the idea the same place he got the one for a quickie biography of Elizabeth Taylor.

Now I was never offered that job, but my good friend Don Westlake was. And Don took it on, did a creditable job of sifting clippings and pasting together something that made

Heckelmann happy, and it was published in due course: *Elizabeth Taylor: A Fascinating Story of America's Most Talented Actress and the World's Most Beautiful Woman,* by John B. Allan. Don never used that pen name before or since, nor did he write any other biographies of actresses. And I don't know that Monarch published any other actress bios, either.

So why did they want this one? Because Ms. Taylor had been ill a lot at the time, and Heckelmann figured there was a good chance she was dying. If she kicked off, well, he wanted to have a book on the stands before the body was cold.

Get the picture? Fidel Castro was neither America's most talented actress or the world's most beautiful woman, but he was very much in the news, and there were rumors—well-founded, it would turn out—that some important and well-placed persons were plotting his assassination. Well, by golly, if someone was going to kill Castro, why shouldn't Monarch make a buck on the deal?

I suppose it was worth a gamble. I got fifteen hundred dollars for the book, and I think Don got about the same for the Taylor opus, and it's not as though either book required its subject's death in order to sell a few copies. And if either long shot came in, well, Heckelmann would look like a genius. A ghoulish genius, but a genius all the same.

Ah well. Last I looked, Fidel and Liz were both still alive. Charlie, on the other hand, died a while back.

It was a challenge, writing the book. I didn't know a whole lot about Cuba, and I was limited to what I could find out at the library because a fifteen hundred dollar advance wasn't going to send me to Havana to do on-the-ground research. And Heckelmann wanted the book in a hell of a hurry. God knows what he'd heard . . .

I wrote it quickly enough, and I happen to know that I finished it on March 29, 1961. How do I remember? Well, if I'd forgotten, the dedication would remind me:

This is for Amy Jo,
who was born yesterday

If I didn't learn all that much about Cuba, I did learn a little about writing—specifically, about writing action scenes, something with which I'd had little experience. And I guess the book came off OK. Here's what a very generous Amazon.com reviewer had to say when Hard Case Crime published the book:

Hard Case Crime has done it again, bringing us a 1961 pseudonymous thriller from Lawrence Block. *Killing Castro* focuses on one member of a ragtag ensemble cast who have accepted a commission to kill Fidel Castro. They begin in Tampa, make their separate ways to Havana and . . . well . . . don't think that later history guarantees that Fidel will make it through the final reel.

The narrative is taut, the language pulpy, the plotting perfect. Drenched in booze, cigarette and cigar smoke, beans and rice and sex, the story moves to its satisfying conclusion. Along the way there are interspersed accounts of Fidel's rise to and abuse of power. And give Block special points for his knowledge of Cuba in general, Havana in particular.

The book underscores Block's persistent and longstanding talent for this sort of writing. He does it now and he could do it then. And, no, hit man Turner in this book is not the prototype for Block's current hit man, John Keller. He's his own man and he's got some dangerous partners. Fidel, watch your back. (Richard B. Schwartz, "Old Reliable," review of *Killing Castro*, by Lawrence Block, Amazon.com, February 10, 2009)

I got another very generous review around the same time from an old friend of mine, long active in leftist circles. "You had the right slant on Cuba all along," she wrote. I did? Well, even a blind sow finds an acorn once in a while

I've written a whole lot of books under a whole lot of names, and there are readers out there who've devoted a lot of time and energy into rooting out this pseudonymous work of mine. I've been credited—if that's the word—with a good many books I had no connection with, but I can think of only two books that no one knew were mine.

Fidel Castro Assassinated was one of them. The pen name— Henry Morrison's selection—was Lee Duncan. Heckelmann may or may not have thought that was the author's real name, but it was the only name he had, and he slapped it on the book and that was that.

Charles Ardai of Hard Case Crime came up with the new title, *Killing Castro*, and I think it's a great improvement. And now, as this fifty-year-old tale bounces around cyberspace as an ebook, I can only sit back and wish it well. And hope you enjoyed it.

LUCKY AT CARDS

Sometime in late 1963 I had a falling-out with my agent. I'd been represented by the Scott Meredith Literary Agency ever since I took employment there as an editor in the summer of 1957. I had left the job and returned to Antioch College after nine or ten months but remained a client of the agency until I chafed at some crap assignment and wound up suddenly agentless. My primary market at the time was Bill Hamling's soft-core operation, Nightstand Books, and it was a closed shop; Scott Meredith (under a deep corporate cover) filled all their editorial needs. I had a wife and a mortgage and two kids under three years old, and no college degree or marketable skills except the ability to make up stories and string words together.

That sounds fairly dire, and I suppose it was, but it was decades later before I realized it didn't have to be. I could have mended the fences. One phone call to Scott, a mumbled apology, and I'd have been back in the fold. In fact there *was* a phone call—*from* Scott—to clear up some unfinished business, and at its conclusion he suggested I return to the fold. And I declined.

Does that sound like a principled stand? Or like wrong-headed obstinacy? I have to say it was neither, just an inability to perceive options. How could I go back to being a client? You know, I always did well on IQ tests and, when I put my mind to it, at schoolwork. But in certain basic respects, I really wasn't terribly bright, was I?

Never mind. I had a living to make, and only one way to make it, and I went to work. I was living in a Buffalo, New York, suburb at the time, out of touch with the world of publishing. We probably should have moved back to New York City, but we stayed put and I worked to develop new markets for myself. I'd written a number of books for Harry Shorten at Midwood Tower, and that was *not* a Scott Meredith closed shop, but did I give Harry a ring and try to set something up? No, never thought of it. Instead I established a new identity as Jill Emerson, wrote a sensitive lesbian novel, and sent it to Midwood as an over-the-transom submission. (They bought it and launched Jill Emerson's checkered career, but that's another story; you'll find it in the afterwords to *Warm & Willing* and *Enough of Sorrow*.)

I'd written some psychosexual nonfiction (made up case histories) for Lancer Books, and I knew Larry T. Shaw well enough to call him up and propose a book. So that was a market. I knew something about coins, and knocked out a book on coin investment that Frederick Fell published. I sold articles to a batch of numismatic (currency) magazines: *Coins*, *Numismatic Scrapbook*, and *The Whitman Numismatic Journal*.

And then there was Beacon.

Before there was Midwood or Nightstand, Beacon Books had essentially created the genre of widely distributed soft-core paperback fiction, with Orrie Hitt their leading writer. I believe *A Diet of Treacle* was my first book for Beacon, although it didn't set out to be; I had more ambitious aims for the book, set in the beat/hip demimonde of Greenwich Village. But when other publishers passed, my agent sent the manuscript to Beacon, where it was published as *Pads Are for Passion* by Sheldon Lord. That was the pen name I'd put on my Midwood titles, and I decided to use it at Beacon as well.

I wrote two more books specifically for Beacon, *April North* and *Community of Women*. The latter was a Beacon editor's idea; he must have been a commuter, given to fantasies about daytime life in his suburb after all the men had caught the 8:02 a.m. train to Grand Central Station.

When the books came out, I made the mistake of having a look at them; when some sentences struck me as unwieldy, I checked my carbon copies. Beacon was a strange publishing house indeed. The publisher, a fellow named Arnold Abramson, came out of the world of pulp magazines and took it as an article of faith that anything he bought from a writer had to be rewritten by an editor. And so he had a whole roomful of editors whose job it was to change the manuscripts they bought, whether they needed it or not. If the editors didn't make abundant changes, they'd be out of a job. So they changed my compound sentences to simple sentences and hooked my simple sentences together as compound sentences and so on, all the way through to the end. They certainly didn't make the stuff better, and I don't suppose they made it a great deal worse, but the whole business annoyed the hell out of me. The pay wasn't all that good, so I figured I'd write for somebody else.

But Beacon wanted more from Sheldon Lord, and Scott Meredith's merry men figured out how to handle that. They enlisted ghostwriters to furnish Sheldon Lord manuscripts, and in return for the use of my name, I got a slice of the advance. Two hundred dollars a book, if I remember correctly.

And how many of these ghostwritten manuscripts were there over a two or three year period? Beats me. Eight or ten, something like that? I didn't know anything about the ghosts and never saw their books or knew what they were writing. One guy was named Milo and one guy wasn't, and my old college buddy Peter Hochstein wrote at least one of the books, with results that were interesting enough to discuss in the afterword to *April North*. But the whole ghosting operation had pretty much stopped by the time Scott Meredith and I parted company.

* * *

I don't think I had Beacon in mind when I wrote *Lucky at Cards*. It's a straight suspense novel, not a soft-core sex opus, and I probably intended it for Gold Medal, where I'd already published *Grifter's Game* and *Coward's Kiss*—albeit under other titles. But I needed a quick sale, and that's probably what made me send the manuscript to Bernie Williams at Beacon.

Well, he loved it. I had lunch with him in New York, and we had this wacky conversation in which he told me how much of an improvement the book was on my recent work for them. It required hardly any editing, he said, and showed me some pages of a recent Sheldon Lord manuscript that had been edited to death. It was comforting to know I was better than the guys who'd been ghosting for me, but it made for a weird moment or two.

Bernie called the book *The Sex Shuffle*, perhaps thinking that the promise of sex might help offset the book's lack of much sexual content. And he did something Beacon has never done before or since, so far as I know: He put a quote on the cover enthusing about the book. The source of the quote was given as one otherwise unidentified "William Bernard," and my keen analytical mind leads me to suspect that it was in fact Bernie Williams.

There was a wonderful moment at that lunch. Bernie had an idea for a book I might write next, one that examined the relationship of an older husband with a much younger wife. "It's almost a cliché in fiction," he said, "but the thing is it's always portrayed negatively. I'd like to see a book in which a marriage like that works out. Because sometimes it does work out. Sometimes a marriage like that can be a huge success."

That was the only time I met Bernie, and I never did meet his wife, whom I'm certain must have been a good twenty years his junior. I can only hope they went on being happy together. He was a nice man, and he bought a book from me when I sorely needed a sale. I never did take a shot at his May-December novel because a fellow named Ken Bressett, who'd bought articles from me for the *Whitman Numismatic Journal*, showed up in Buffalo and offered me a job. We sold the house and moved to Racine, Wisconsin.

Years later, Charles Ardai snapped up *The Sex Shuffle*, restored its original title, *Lucky at Cards*, and published it at Hard Case Crime. Here's a review from *Publishers Weekly*: "The Hard Case Crime imprint has found a perfect partner in Block, as this gritty grifter's tale, in print for the first time in forty years, goes to show . . . The plot twists here, then there, then back again, rooted in Block's strong characters and no-nonsense prose style."

And here's another from Bill Tot in *Booklist*:

Before Matt Scudder, before Bernie Rhodenbarr, before being named a Mystery Writers of America Grand Master, Lawrence Block turned out paperback originals. This one—unavailable for more than forty years—now receives a timely reissue from Hard Case Crime. It's a doozy . . . Block unwinds his plot superbly, pointing toward a classic noir finale but then seeming to pull away—or maybe not. And, along the way, there is all the teasing sexuality and tongue-in-cheek noir style that a pulp devotee craves.

The book probably owes a little to *The Tooth and the Nail*, by Bill S. Ballinger, a fine writer who's pretty much forgotten these days. Let's hope he's rediscovered. If *Lucky at Cards* can have a new life as an ebook after all these years, well, anything's possible, isn't it?

NOT COMIN' HOME TO YOU

Not Comin' Home to You was the third and last book I published under the pen name of Paul Kavanagh. The first, *Such Men Are Dangerous*, was purportedly narrated by its author, a burnt-out CIA operative–turned-recluse; the second, *The Triumph of Evil*, was a third-person novel of political suspense featuring a Central European assassin. *Not Comin' Home to You* is a work of fiction inspired by, but not too closely patterned after, a real-life murder spree that took place some fifteen years earlier in Nebraska.

It's hard to see what Paul Kavanagh's three works have in common, aside from fitting under the broad canopy of crime fiction. I've speculated in the afterword for *The Triumph of Evil* as to what my reasons may have been for writing under pen names, so I'll spare you a reprise of that; suffice it to say that the three Kavanagh novels, at the time of their writing, were the books I viewed as my most serious attempts.

Charles Starkweather and Caril Ann Fugate killed a batch of Nebraskans, including her family, in 1958. About ten years later I thought of making something out of it, and I saw it as source material not for a novel but for a film. At the time the only screenwriting I'd done had been a draft for a producer who'd optioned one of my Tanner books. Nothing had ever come of that, but I discussed my new idea with my agent and wrote a treatment (essentially an outline) for the proposed film. I sent it to my agent, and he shopped it around, and nobody cared. I had other things to do and I did them.

I had written the screen treatment in the attic of a house in New Brunswick, New Jersey, and I didn't think about it again until we'd spent a couple of years in a farmhouse near Lambertville. I realized that what hadn't gone anywhere as a screenplay could be a novel, and as I recall I wrote it in a couple of weeks of fairly intense effort. I'd been in the habit of writing my books in New York, in one of a series of pieds-à-terre I kept for that purpose, but toward the end of my time in that house I finally started doing some writing there.

I didn't have a den or study but there was a splendid Jacobean refectory table in our dining room, and I wrote *Not Comin' Home to You* at that table, starting work late at night when the rest of the family was asleep. I suspect the fallow years since I'd written the treatment had been useful ones; my unconscious had had plenty of time to figure out what to make of the story, and it was very real for me as I wrote it.

I deliberately set the story in present time—the early seventies—and deliberately avoided the facts of the case and the actual life histories and personalities of the real-life killers. I figured the hell with all that. This was a novel and needed to be reimagined altogether.

I showed it to my agent, and he showed it to Clyde Taylor at G. P. Putnam's Sons publishing. I'd called it *Just a Couple of Kids*. Clyde didn't care for that and suggested I use the title of a song I'd written for the book. I went along with it because he was the editor and I wanted to keep him happy. But I don't think it was the right title. *Kids* would have been better. Or *Just Kids*. Or, I dunno, something.

Both Clyde and I were optimistic about the book's possibilities, not only in bookstores but on the screen. Then, shortly before book publication, Terrence Malick's film *Badlands* was released, starring Martin Sheen and Sissy Spacek as Starkweather and Fugate. That killed any chance of a film sale.

When I saw the movie, I felt ill-used. I certainly didn't have any proprietary hold on the source material and it wasn't unlikely that someone else would be similarly inspired, but my screen treatment had been shown around a couple of years before the movie was made and there was a scene in my treatment that I'd invented out of whole cloth.

In my treatment, and again in *Not Comin' Home to You*, the two killers take refuge in a vacant farmhouse, and have a little domestic interlude during which they are decent, nonviolent people who even take pains to leave the premises in good condition before they move on to resume their killing spree. Now this never happened and nothing like it ever happened, but I thought it would be a nice dramatic touch.

And so did Terrence Malick, evidently; there's a similar interlude in *Badlands*, in which the two build a sort of tree house complex, lashing poles together. (They construct in a couple of hours what would take anybody else two or three weeks, but that's Hollywood.) At the time, I was certain whoever was responsible for that scene had read my treatment and plucked the idea out of it, and I had fantasies of being introduced to Malick at a party, say, and decking the sonofabitch.

I never did run into the man, but if I ever do, I have to say he's safe from my wrath. He probably thought up the scene the same way I did, recognizing that it would work dramatically and that the storyline called for that sort of a break.

Irish Alzheimer's is what they call it when you find yourself forgetting resentments. I would appear to be in its early stages.

A word or two about the song. I wrote it for the book and

then used it as an epigraph. While the book was "by Paul Kavanagh," the song was credited to me, Lawrence Block.

When I finished the book, my wife read it—she didn't read everything I wrote, but she read this. I'd decided I was going to dedicate it to my three daughters, but she made an uncharacteristic request: Would I dedicate this one to her? That seemed reasonable enough, and I amended the dedication accordingly:

> *To my daughters*
> *Amy, Jill, and Alison*
> *and to their mother.*

The marriage, which had almost ended six years earlier, crashed permanently in the summer of 1973. I moved back to the city and my agent Henry Morrison placed the book with Clyde Taylor. I kept Clyde happy by agreeing to his title. And so a book called *Not Comin' Home to You* bore the dedication quoted earlier.

And then about a year after the book came out, a fellow got in touch with me. He was a pianist and composer and voice coach who he lived on the Upper West Side, and his first name was Mack. (I'll be damned if I can remember his last name, and Google seems incapable of helping me out. I last heard from him in 1977; he was playing piano for a Broadway show, and we met for a drink in the upstairs bar at Sardi's. An awfully nice fellow, and I'm sorry we lost touch.)

He contacted me in the first place because he had a young singer he was coaching. He'd picked up my novel, read the lyric, and thought it would be a great song for her. He'd actually written a tune for it, and she'd been working on it and wanted to include it on a demo album, but for all he knew it already had a melody, and might even be recorded, and—

Well, it wasn't and it hadn't, and it was all fine with me. I met him and met her and even went to the recording session. I'd written it as a country song, and his was more of a rock version, but it sounded OK.

Nothing ever came of it. I've long since forgotten her name, and I don't know if she ever had a career, but if she did, my song's not what got her started.

Strange where things lead you, and where they don't. If this rings a bell with any of y'all out there in ebook country, let me know about it. I don't really expect to hear from Mack at this late date, or from the singer (an attractive girl, with a good voice), but it could happen. Stranger things do, all the time.

RANDOM WALK

Say someone comes up to me at a signing and says something like this: "I've been reading your books for years and I've always enjoyed them, but there was this one novel of yours and I swear I couldn't make head or tail out of it, and—" And I know right away he's talking about *Random Walk*.

Or perhaps what he says is more along the lines of, "I've been reading your books for years and I always enjoy them, but there's one book of yours that I read seventeen times and it changed my life and—" And once again the book in question always turns out to be *Random Walk*.

I grant you it's an odd one. Guy in Roseburg, Oregon, quits his bartending job for no apparent reason and starts walking east across the Cascades. Other people are drawn to him and the group generates its own mysterious energy, and Things Happen.

Meanwhile, a real estate developer in Kansas starts driving all over the Midwest, killing women for pleasure. Uh, that'd be his pleasure, not theirs.

Writing it was a remarkable experience. I was living in Florida at the time, and I got this image of a guy walking across the country. And, over the next several days, other characters began revealing themselves to me. I had time booked at a writers' colony in Virginia and had to go there right away and Write Away. But this was going to be a remarkably complex story, with dozens of characters and intricate plot threads, so it would have to wait.

Except it couldn't, because how could I think about anything else when I was thinking about this story all the time? So I went to the writers' colony figuring I could do some outlining and instead I sat down and wrote twenty pages a day for twenty-three days, and when I was done so was the book. It didn't feel like taking down Celestial Dictation; I was very much the one in charge, making decisions every day. But all I knew was what I'd write that day, and somehow the next morning I was given to know what to write *that* day. And so on.

A wonderful experience, let me tell you. *Random Walk* was a book that clearly wanted to be written. However, it turned out to be a book that didn't much want to be read, and hardly anybody read it.

The book got lousy reviews back in 1988, and the publisher didn't make much of an effort, and it pretty much vanished without a trace. (The original cover looked sort of sci-fi-ish. The cover of the paperback looked like a novel of the western migration. No wonder nobody bought it in either form.)

I brought the book back via iUniverse some years ago, and

now it's an ebook and it goes on finding its audience. Of which you are now a part; I can only hope you enjoyed it.

RONALD RABBIT IS A DIRTY OLD MAN

James T. Seels
ASAP Press
Mission Viejo CA

Dear Jim,

First, I want to tell you how enthusiastic I am about your publication of *Ronald Rabbit Is a Dirty Old Man.* It's been out of print in all editions forever, as you know. As a matter of fact, it was barely in print to begin with.

I know I promised you an introduction for the new edition, and I wouldn't mind taking a trip down Memory Lane and filling a few pages with the sort of nattering typical of aging writers as they recall their presumably carefree youth. (Mine, actually, was not so much carefree as it was careless.) I've written a slew of intros and afterwords in the past few years as various youthful indiscretions of mine have been reissued by specialty publishers, and I think I've got the knack of it by now.

In the present instance, though, I've had trouble getting a grip on it, perhaps because I've got all too many demands on my time and energy. I just got back a scant week ago from a book tour, I'm having lunch tomorrow to plan another tour three months from now, I'm working away on a new book with a deadline that's not all that far off, I have to revise a two hour teleplay with an even closer deadline, and the next three months are peppered with speaking dates and interviews and conferences. Along with everything else, I'm on the StairMonster every day trying heroically to climb out of the Pit of Doom, and I'm wasting no end of time *on-line*, and how am I going to find the time to write this intro and make it interesting?

Damned if I know. Maybe if I just write my thoughts to you in this letter, I'll get some clarity on the whole thing.

So here goes. In 1969 I moved to a country place near Lambertville, New Jersey, with my then-wife and still-daughters. We'd bought a rambling farmhouse that contained everything but a place to write. Besides, I couldn't seem to get any writing done there. There was a goat to milk and a garden to tend and growing things to look at. The first six months I lived there I couldn't get a word written. Then I came into the city and took a hotel room on West Forty-fourth Street, and I wrote a book in a week.

Hmmmm, I thought.

So for the rest of my sojourn in the country, that's how I worked it. When it was time to write, I would come to town. At first I used the hotel, and then I shared a pied-à-terre with Brian Garfield, who was also living in Jersey with his then-wife. Finally, I moved to an apartment on West Thirty-fifth Street between Fifth and Sixth Avenues. It was on the top floor of a small building, four flights up from Drum's Restaurant. (Drum owned the building. He's gone now, and so's his restaurant. The building's still there.)

I didn't have the apartment that long, but it seems

to me I wrote a lot of books there. The second Chip Harrison novel, *Chip Harrison Scores Again*. A political thriller, *The Triumph of Evil*, which was my second book under the pen name Paul Kavanagh. A couple of books of nonfiction, sexual case histories published under a pen name you don't really need to know.

And *Ronald Rabbit*.

It's not much of a secret that I wrote a lot of adult novels early in my career. (God knows why they call them that. It's the ultimate euphemism, isn't it? An adult novel is one no genuine adult would bother with.) They were mostly pretty tame by contemporary standards, and they certainly weren't very good. I started writing them in 1958, and kept at it for five years.

In the late sixties, though, I was struck by the urge to explore the form again, if you want to call it that. But I didn't want to grind out monthly trash the way I'd done earlier. I wanted to write some frankly erotic books that would be fun to write and might even be interesting to a reader with a three-figure IQ. My agent found an enthusiastic publisher, and I did three books in all, publishing them under a female pen name, one I'd used earlier on a pair of lesbian novels.

Ronald Rabbit was initially intended as a pseudonymous paperback original. I wanted to write an epistolary novel but not the traditional series of narrative letters from a single character in the manner of Samuel Richardson's *Pamela*. Instead I was inspired by Mark Harris's brilliant comic soufflé *Wake Up, Stupid*, and my good friend Hal Dresner's hilarious *The Man Who Wrote Dirty Books*. Each tells its story through the medium of the collected correspondence of the protagonist, letters written to him as well as letters written by him, and that's what I wanted to do in *Ronald Rabbit*.

Beyond that, what did I know about *Ronald Rabbit* when I sat down to begin it? Well, I had for inspiration the example of a fellow I knew from a poker game I played in once a week. He had of late been let go (with generous severance pay and continuing medical coverage) six months after the magazine he edited had ceased publication. Like Laurence Clarke, he managed to stay so long because nobody noticed he was there. And I drew additional inspiration from the example of another fellow who played in that same game, a married writer who got drunk one night on Macdougal Street and wound up riding clear back to Noroton, Connecticut, in a station wagon full of girls from a very prestigious convent school.

When God gives you all that to work with, it shouldn't be all that hard to produce a novel.

Nor was it. I wrote *Ronald Rabbit* in four days. They were, it must be said, long days—not because I was in a great rush to get done, but because I couldn't seem to stop. One letter kept leading to another. I was completely caught up in the realization of the havoc that could be wreaked by a single manipulative maniac with a typewriter, and I just kept hammering away at it, and in hardly any time at all I was done.

Then I got various friends to read it because I had the feeling it ought not waste its fragrance upon the desert air of pseudonymous paperbackery. Everybody chose to confirm me in this folly, and my agent pledged the book with Bernard Geis, and I thought I was going to get rich. For years I'd scratched out a meager living by writing dirty books under pen names. Now I had broken through. I had written a dirty book under my own name, and the world was sure to be my oyster.

Except, of course, it didn't turn out that way. Geis, who'd written several great chapters in the history of contemporary publishing, picked that moment to write Chapter Eleven. It didn't take an astrologer to see it was not the best time to be published by him. He tried, and there was actually an ad, and he had a ton of promotional campaign buttons printed, but the book essentially sank without a trace.

Rumors of lucrative reprint deals came and went, too, and finally my agent called to tell me that Manor Books wanted to do the book in paperback. They would pay a hot fifteen hundred dollars, all of which would go to Geis to offset some of the unearned balance of the five thousand dollar advance he'd given me.

Some oyster.

There was a catch, though. Manor wanted to change the title. I told them no.

Geis called my agent. "Talk some sense into Larry," he said. "If he won't let them change the title, it might queer the deal."

"God," I said, "I hope so." But it didn't. Manor published the book in paperback, with the original title, and their edition is probably harder to find than Geis's hardcover edition. The only other edition the book has ever had is a Japanese one, and that may be the hardest of all to find, because how would I even know if I found it?

So there you have it, Jim. That's how the book came about. And you know what else it is? It's the intro. Just copy this letter directly as the introduction to your sumptuous edition. What better intro to a book of letters than another letter? In fact you might want to photograph this letter rather than bother setting type. Don't worry about the letterhead. I've already changed the phone number to one of those generic 555 nonexistent numbers, and I don't care if the rest is public information. If people want to write me letters or send me faxes, I say God bless 'em.

Hang in there, Jim. And be nice, or I'll get Laurence Clarke after you.

And let me add, Dear E-Reader, how pleased I am to have *Ronald Rabbit* available as an ebook. I can only hope you had a fraction of the fun reading it that I had writing it.

THE SPECIALISTS

My novel *The Specialists* was published as a paperback original by Gold Medal Books. Some years later, James Cahill published a first hardcover edition of the book and requested that I furnish an introduction. Here's what I found to say about the book: I suppose it's fair to say that I'm most often identified as the creator of series characters. My two active series, concerning a bookselling burglar named Rhodenbarr and a sober drunk named Scudder, are the ones people are most likely to know about. Readers with a wider range may be familiar as well with a series of seven novels about an insomniac named Tanner, and another series of four novels about a horny kid named Harrison.

A relative handful will have followed the adventures in short-story form of two other gents, an attorney called Ehrengraf and a killer named Keller. But that's about as far as it goes. Hardly anybody, asked to name all of my series, would come up with *The Specialists*.

A fat lot they know. As far as I'm concerned, *The Specialists* is unequivocally a series novel. As it happens, the series is only one book long. But I figure it's a series just the same.

What on earth is he talking about, Maude?

Easy, there. I can explain.

In the spring of 1966 I moved into a big old house on a small old lot smack in the middle of New Brunswick, New Jersey. I set up an office for myself on the third floor. I had a massive old desk, and the movers couldn't get the thing up the last flight of stairs. It wouldn't fit. Most desks of that vintage disassemble, but not this sucker. They had to cut the back legs off it. I propped up the back of the desk with two short stacks of paperback novels, plopped a typewriter on top of it, and went to work.

Three and a half years later, when we moved to a place in the country, I left the desk right there, and I left the books to keep it from tilting. By that time the desk didn't owe me a dime, because I'd sat at it and written a whole slew of books. I'd already written the first Tanner book in Racine, Wisconsin, but I wrote the other six in New Brunswick, along with *After the First Death* and *Such Men Are Dangerous* and more pseudonymous work than I'll admit to at the moment. (I wrote *No Score*, the first Chip Harrison novel, in that house but not on that desk. I moved downstairs to the first floor and wrote it on the breakfast-room table. I can't remember why.)

I also wrote *The Specialists* at that desk. My then-agent (and still-friend) Henry Morrison suggested I might try to come up with a series, and he liked the idea of a group of guys working together in the tried-and-true manner of *The League of Gentlemen*. I hadn't read the book in question, but I got the idea. I wrote a couple of chapters and an outline and pitched the idea as a series to an editor at (I think) Dell Publishing. Whoever she was and wherever she was, she thought the outline sounded good, and I went home to my desk to finish the first book.

And I did, and you in turn have read it . . . unless you're one of those people who read the afterword first and then read the book. If you're of a more conventional temperament, you may have noticed how very much a part of a series it is. I did all the series things, did them with considerable calculation. I dropped in tantalizing little references to past adventures, figuring we'd hear more about them later on. I gave the characters back stories I could build on and play off of in future books. I did all kinds of things along those lines because it was quite clear to me that I wasn't writing a novel, I was writing the first installment of a series. My deal with Dell (or whoever it was), when we finalized it, would be for three books, and who knew how many I'd wind up writing? My guys could go on having adventures until their gruff old colonel grew himself a new leg. Hell, I could write about these bozos forever!

Yeah, right.

I finished the book without a problem, and Henry liked it, and he sent it over to Dell. (I *think* it was Dell.) While I'd been breezing along on the book, the editor who'd liked the idea had gone somewhere else, and her replacement didn't like the idea— or the book, either. Henry took it back and sent it to Knox Burger at Gold Medal Books, who had published a number of books of mine, and who liked it just fine. I signed a contract and then I got a call from Henry.

"Knox was wondering," he said, "if *The Specialists* is the first volume of a series. Shall I tell him yes, and that you're already hard at work on the next installment?"

"God, no," I said.

"Huh?"

"Tell him it's complete in and of itself," I said.

"But I thought—"

"So did I," I said, "and it turns out we were both wrong. Because I like the book and I sort of enjoyed writing it, but when I finished it I realized something. I don't want to write about those guys again, ever. I liked them as characters, and it's the kind of book I like to read, but it turns out it's not the kind of book I like to *write*."

There was a pause. Then Henry said, "That's really strange."

"I know it is."

"I was sure it was going to turn out to be a series."

"So was I, and we were right. It's a series. But it's a very short series."

"Just one book long."

"Just one book long," I agreed. "But a series nonetheless."

And that's what it is. I hope you enjoyed it. I like it, I must admit, and I'm happy to see it in print in such a handsome edition. I'm glad you've got it on your shelf, and I'm happy to have it on *my* shelf.

And who knows? Maybe someday I *will* want to write about those guys again . . .

Well now. Jim Cahill's edition has long since gone out of print, and I still haven't written further about the Colonel and his merry band. But *The Specialists* is available again, now as an ebook, and I'm not half chuffed to see my one-book series find a new cyberaudience for itself.

Hmmm. You know, maybe I *should* write more about the lads . . .

SUCH MEN ARE DANGEROUS

"This will sock you right between the eyes. It's terrific!"
—*Publishers Weekly*
"Goes through you like a dose of salts and stings like iodine."
—*Kirkus Reviews*

Hmmm. I rather hope the experience of reading *Such Men Are Dangerous* isn't quite the exercise in masochism these two reviewers make it out to be. I need all the readers I can get, and wouldn't want to leave them all punched out, purged, and stung to a fare-thee-well.

Still, it's nice to think the book might have an impact.

The book came about at a curious time in my own life, and one I've never been inclined to write about. But the afterwords I've been dashing off, designed to accompany my early work into an extended life in the cyberworld of epublishing, have sent me careening down memory lane, bouncing from pothole to pothole, and I might as well keep at it. And if I am indeed writing an extended inchoate memoir on the installment plan, well, so be it.

"A curious time in my own life." Yes, I guess we can call it that.

In 1966, after an eighteen-month foray into the corporate world at Western Printing in Racine, Wisconsin, my wife and two daughters and I relocated to New Brunswick, New Jersey. My career had taken a turn for the better in Wisconsin; I'd written several books while I was there, most recently the first Tanner adventure, to be published as *The Thief Who Couldn't Sleep*, and now had Henry Morrison as my agent. (Henry and I had worked side by side at the Scott Meredith Literary Agency in 1957–8, and he handled my work until Scott and I parted company. A year or two after that, he left Scott's employ and set up on his own shop. In due course he got in touch with me, and it was he who placed Tanner with Gold Medal Books.)

Within a year, however, everything had pretty much gone to hell.

How to put it? Bluntly, I suppose, and at the same time obliquely. A very close friend and colleague was having an affair with the widow of another friend and colleague. And, sometime late in 1966, my friend's girlfriend and I discovered, to our considerable excitement, that we were right up there with Richard Burton and Elizabeth Taylor, if not Dante and Beatrice. We had an affair that could not have been less decorous had our liaisons been staged in Macy's window. My friend and I both separated from our wives, and there were some appalling scenes, public and private. And I went back to my wife and back to the other woman, and so on, until I felt as though I were the battered shuttlecock in a drunken game of badminton.

So I went to Ireland to regroup. I finished a Tanner book— *Tanner's Twelve Swingers,* begun in New Jersey and completed in Dublin and set, of course, in Latvia. I was in Ireland for two months, and thinking of living there permanently, until I woke up one day in West Cork with a hangover that impressed even the locals. I flew home from Shannon and moved back in with my wife, and I hadn't been home an hour before I knew it wouldn't work. And it didn't, though we were together another six years or so.

Meanwhile, my friend and his wife got a divorce, and he married the girlfriend. That didn't work, either.

In West Cork, before the hangover, I'd felt about as hopeless as it was possible to feel, and in my inn's library I came upon Graham Greene's *A Burnt-Out Case*, which seemed then to have been written with me in mind. What I got from it was the insight that when one can't go on, what one does is go on. So on I went, living again in New Brunswick, and trying to get something written. I'd started another Tanner book in Ireland—*The Scoreless Thai*—and I finished that, and then I sat around for a couple of months doing nothing much. We had a big round mahogany table in the dining room, American Empire in style, and I would sit there all day playing solitaire. Some nights I'd drink. Some nights I wouldn't. It didn't seem to make much difference.

I didn't write anything because I couldn't see the point. I just got through the days—playing solitaire, reading, drinking. Time passed. It always does.

Then one day I went upstairs and started writing the book that turned out to be *Such Men Are Dangerous*. I wrote all day every day for a week, went to New York for two days, then came back and wrote for two more days, and that was that. The book was done.

Well, it's not hard to guess where the protagonist came from. Paul Kavanagh and I didn't have a lot of life experience in common, but somehow we'd reached the same internal place.

That's probably as much as you need to know about the writing of *Such Men Are Dangerous*, and as much as I need to tell you. But I probably ought to say something about the frame device; the book purports to be a true story written by the person who lived it. (Although I began putting my own name on the book years ago, it was initially published "by Paul Kavanagh".) I'm not entirely sure why I chose to do it that way. It was a book I was pleased with, and it would have certainly done my career no harm to have it appear under my own name, but the gamesmanship of it probably appealed to me. I don't know, and after all these years I don't suppose it matters.

I don't know that I really thought anyone would buy the premise, but I actually received a letter, sent to my publisher and dutifully forwarded to me, from a chap who ran some sort of charity in the UK. He'd noted that all royalties from the book were to be given to charity, and he respectfully proposed his worthy organization to be the recipient of some if not all of the funds.

One more story. Sometime in the mid-eighties, a good fifteen years after the novel was published, I was married again and living in the West Village. My wife Lynne had some people over to the house, and one of them, a former CIA employee, spotted a copy of *Such Men* on a table.

"Oh, I know about that book," the guy said. "A Company guy wrote it."

"No," Lynne said. "That's one of my husband's books."

"Yeah, right," the fellow said. "Look, everybody at the Company knew about that guy. Wandered off the reservation, pulled some weird shit. That's the book he wrote."

THE TRIUMPH OF EVIL

The Triumph of Evil was the second book I published under the pen name of Paul Kavanagh.

Now there was an excuse for the first one, although I'm not sure it was a very good one. Paul Kavanagh was not only the putative author of *Such Men Are Dangerous;* he was also its protagonist and first-person narrator. I'm sure virtually all of the book's readers recognized that it was a novel and that it had been written by a professional writer of fiction whose name was almost certainly something other than Paul Kavanagh. Still, it was a way for the book to present itself and at least a tenuous reason to employ a pseudonym.

But *The Triumph of Evil* was a third-person novel, and its protagonist was world-weary European agent and assassin named Miles Dorn. The book was a novel of political suspense, by no means categorically dissimilar to the books I was writing under my own name, so why slap Paul Kavanagh's name on it?

It's not as though the Kavanagh lad had a following. *Such Men* got some good reviews but it didn't set the world on fire, and Paul Kavanagh's name on a book wouldn't cause it to fly off the shelves.

So why the pen name?

Why any pen names, ever?

Well, I don't suppose it's hard to grasp why I might have wanted to use names other than my own on the books I wrote for Nightstand Books and Midwood Tower and Beacon Books. The houses occupied the lowest echelon of paperback publishing, and the books I published with them were soft-core erotica. They are quite tame by today's standards, but they were as determinedly erotic as the times allowed. It wouldn't astonish me to learn that a bookseller here and there may have gone to jail on my account.

I wasn't worried about going to jail. I was probably more afraid of being forever overlooked, but I didn't want my name on books that were categorically third-rate. I wasn't ashamed of the books I published as Sheldon Lord and Andrew Shaw. I was, if anything, proud that I could produce publishable work, proud that I could make a living doing so. The books did what they were trying to do, but their sights were set low. My own name, I felt, ought to be reserved for something more ambitious. And almost everybody else in the business seemed to feel the same way.

I also wrote purported nonfiction, books on sexual topics featuring fabricated case histories, and I used pen names on those books as well. Two of the names had *M.D.* after them— you can do that, I was assured, as long as you neither diagnose nor prescribe. I never did either, nor did I yank out anybody's appendix. Is it any wonder I didn't put my own name on those books?

The very first book I wrote, *Strange Are the Ways of Love,* had to have a pen name on it. It was a lesbian novel, and you couldn't publish a lesbian novel with a man's name on the cover. That'd be just a little too butch for the market. I liked that book just fine, I'd have been proud to have the world know who wrote it, but that wasn't an option. And, when I wrote some more lesbian novels a few years later, I became Jill Emerson to do so.

But, uh, we were talking about *The Triumph of Evil,* weren't we?

Well, yes, I suppose we were. And I think I know why I was Paul Kavanagh for that book, and why I used other pen names when there was no reason to do so.

For a while, when someone asked me that question, I had an answer I could trot out. I'd sigh and I'd shrug, and I'd go on to explain that I'd evidently been trying to avoid building a following.

But I don't think that's it, not really. I wasn't afraid of success, and I wasn't striving to hold it at bay.

I think I found pen names liberating.

This is me, the writer of fiction announces, over and over again. *This is me . . . but it's not.*

Some novelists make their own lives the source material for their work. Other channel their true selves through their imagination, becoming other people who lead other lives in the pages of their work. I have always been of the second sort, and I seem to have found it doubly comforting not only to write about nonexistent people but also to write about them as a nonexistent person myself.

Thus Paul Kavanagh, protagonist of one book, author of another (and, later still, another: *Not Comin' Home to You*.)

A few years passed and I wrote a book that dealt for the first time with the world in which I grew up, the middle-class Jewish community of Buffalo, New York. I didn't tell my story, or that of anyone I knew, and in fact I made my protagonist a woman and published the book under a female pen name. My publisher argued forcefully for me to use my own name on the book, but I wouldn't have it, insisting that a novel about a woman ought to carry a woman's name.

That may or may not have been true; I've discussed it more in the afterword for the book in question, *A Week as Andrea Benstock*, but what difference does it make? It was beside the point. I wanted a pen name because I wanted a pen name.

This is me. But it's not.

I ought to say *something* about *The Triumph of Evil*. It was written during a time of great political paranoia, in the wake of a string of assassinations, and its characters and incidents and overall storyline very much reflect that time. There were more than a few thrillers back then that involved elaborate conspiracies, but I found myself drawn more to the compelling notion of one skilled and resourceful individual acting alone, and changing the political landscape in the process.

The book was written in a very short period of time. A couple of weeks, if I remember correctly. I wrote it in a studio apartment at 21 West Thirty-fifth Street, four flights above Drum's Restaurant. A Mr. Drum owned the restaurant, and the building, too. The restaurant's gone now, and I imagine Drum's gone along with it.

I lived near Lambertville, New Jersey, at the time, with my wife and daughters and a slew of rabbits and donkeys and goats. It was paradise out there, but I couldn't get any writing done. So I came into the city to write, and the various pieds-à-terre I found served as useful venues for adultery.

But I got a lot more writing done than messing around. I wrote *Chip Harrison Scores Again* on West Thirty-Fifth Street as well as *Ronald Rabbit is a Dirty Old Man* and *The Triumph of Evil*. Old Man Drum is gone, and so are two women who briefly brightened my life on West Thirty-Fifth Street, and I wish them all a peaceful repose. But I'm still here, and, remarkably, so are the books. It's hard to know how a work as much of its time as *The Triumph of Evil* holds up all these years later, but I'm glad it's still around, and can only hope you enjoyed it.

YOU COULD CALL IT MURDER

The second book to be published under my own name was *Coward's Kiss,* which its publishers had the great wit to retitle *Death Pulls a Doublecross*. In the afterword to that book's e-edition, I explain how the book grew out of an assignment to write a tie-in novel based on *Markham*, a television series starring Ray Milland, who I must say was cut out for better things.

Well, so was I—and so, as it turned out, was *Coward's Kiss*. My agent and I felt the book I wrote deserved to be more than a tie-in novel, and an editor at Gold Medal Books agreed. We changed the characters' names and that was that.

Except I still had a book to write. Belmont Books had arranged to pay me a thousand dollars to write that tie-in for them, and I had in fact already received half the advance, so what was I going to do? Stiff them? That wouldn't be nice. Pay them back? That wouldn't be sane.

Obviously, all I could do was write the book. And I couldn't let the fact that I'd already written it once stand in my way.

I don't recall much about the experience of writing *Markham*—which is what I called the manuscript at the time, and what Belmont called it, along with a subtitle: *The Case of the Pornographic Photos*. It seems to me I must have started work on it as soon as I finished *Coward's Kiss*, but I first may have taken a week or so to write my monthly volume for Bill Hamling at Nightstand Books.

I was living at 110 West Sixty-ninth Street at the time. I had gotten married in March of 1960, and by the end of the year we had a child on the way and moved to larger quarters uptown. So I wrote about Roy Markham sometime in the summer or fall of 1960, and we moved to 444 Central Park West in December; in March my daughter Amy was born. Some months after that, *Markham* was published, subtitle and all, and the first I knew of it was when I got a phone call late one night from a writer friend of mine named Randall P. Garrett.

Now Randy lived substantially less than a mile from us, around 110th Street and Broadway, and when he wasn't home working he was around the corner in a neighborhood saloon. But that night he called me from Boston. I don't know what got him to Boston. (Well, duh, a train, but why'd he go there? That was never explained.) What Randy had called to tell me, quite out of the blue, was that he had picked up a copy of *Markham,* and that he'd read it in one sitting and thought it was just plain wonderful.

I don't think Randy had ever called me before, and I doubt he'd ever read anything of mine before, either. I recounted the incident to my friend Don Westlake, who guessed that sooner or later Randy would hit me up for a small loan and was laying the groundwork in the meantime. Never happened. While Randy and I crossed paths a few more times before he disappeared into the Pacific time zone, he never phoned again, never said anything about *Markham* or anything else I'd written, and never tried to borrow so much as subway fare.

He was a very interesting fellow, Randy Garrett. Back then, before it became clear that democracy was best served by a drunken electorate, the bars in New York City were required to close on Election Day. Everyone knew where to find Randy on the first Tuesday in November. He'd be in the cocktail lounge of the United Nations, the only place of public accommodation within the five boroughs where liquor could be legally sold.

What Randy mostly wrote when I knew him was science fiction. He went on to make a reputation as a writer of alternate history and is best known for the Lord Darcy novels, in which a Plantagenet dynasty survives into the twentieth century and magic is scientifically established. I haven't read the Lord Darcy books but understand they're rich in puns and wordplay, and I don't find that hard to believe, because I never met anyone as gifted at rhyming or "punnery" as Randy.

He was, during our acquaintance, a High Church Anglican, and met regularly for spiritual counseling with a canon of the church. Sometimes he told the canon jokes, and once wondered if perhaps a joke he'd just told was too risqué for the clergyman's ears. "Oh, your jokes are all right," the man said. "Besides, I can always us them as fodder for my sermons."

"It's a wise canon that knows his own fodder," Randy replied immediately.

Now how the hell did he do that? The more you think about it, the more remarkable the joke becomes.

Randy, an accomplished versifier, took as a personal challenge the fact that true rhymes don't exist for the words *orange* or *silver*, and he furnished a pair of quatrains to remedy the situation:

> Oh, I ate a poisoned orange
> And I know I'll soon be dead
> For I keep on seeing more ang-
> elic forms around my bed.

Or:

> "Though my hair has turned to silver,"
> Said George Washington with pride,
> "Everybody knows I'm still ver-
> acity personified."

Genius, I say. Sheer genius. And to think that a man capable of such wordsmanship called me up to tell me he liked my book!

He was, I feel I must add, the only person ever to say anything nice about *Markham*.

Now this makes it sound as though the book is terrible, or as though people thought it was terrible. And it may be and they may have, but nobody ever told me so. As far as I know, Randy Garrett's the only person who ever read it.

Belmont published it quietly, but then that's the only way they ever published anything. The TV show to which it was tied proved a frail bond indeed, canceled after a single season and off the airways before the book was on the stands.

It must have been twenty years later when Lou Kannenstine, who'd resuscitated the four Chip Harrison books as two double volumes, cast about looking for other works of mine to reprint under his Foul Play Press imprint. One that I suggested was *Markham*, and we agreed that the title would have to go and could take its lame subtitle along with it. But what, he wondered, would I want to title it?

"Hmmm," I said, or words to that effect. I hadn't read the book since I'd written it. "Well, let me think, Lou. You could call it, uh—"

"Just a minute, I didn't catch all of that. Let me write it down. *'You Could Call It—'*"

There was a thought. I'd just been sputtering, but maybe what I'd been sputtering could morph into a title. But what was the book about? I couldn't remember the plot, except that there were photos in it, and dirty ones at that, if the subtitle were to be believed. But there had to be something else, didn't there?

Like a murder, for instance.

"Murder," I said.

"*You Could Call It Murder.* I like it."

"Well, I'm glad," I said. "Because a lot of thought went into it."

Lawrence Block Series

Chip Harrison Series

NO SCORE

No Score is the first of four novels featuring Chip Harrison, and they all bore the lead character's byline when they first appeared as Fawcett paperbacks. The working title of *No Score* was "The Lecher in the Rye," which sums it up well enough; it's a picaresque account of a young man's desperate attempt to become sexually experienced.

Fawcett did very well with the book, and a couple of years later I wrote a sequel. And, because I liked the voice, I wanted to write a third book, but how many times could one lad lose his virginity? So in the third book I put him to work for a private detective, and books three and four are mysteries, and could be called Nero Wolfe pastiches.

In 1984 Countryman Press reprinted *No Score* and *Chip Harrison Scores Again* in a double volume, and asked the ideal person to write an afterword:

Some Afterthoughts
by Hilton Crofield

I don't know why they asked me to write this. Somebody's original brilliant idea was for me to write an introduction to the new edition of *No Score* and *Chip Harrison Scores Again*, and I said okay. Don't ask me why. Then somebody else got the bright idea of calling the double volume Introducing Chip Harrison, which meant that I would be saddled with the job of introducing Introducing Chip Harrison, and I said that, if you really want to know, I'd rather go into the bathroom and squeeze a pimple. So they said okay, we'll make it an afterword, and I said okay again. Don't ask me why. It's not as if I was getting paid for this.

Chip Harrison needs no introduction, and I don't suppose he needs an afterword either, so you can stop reading right now. . . . If you're still with me, I just want to tell you that these are my kind of book. Chip Harrison is a sort of a lecher on the wry side. More than that, when you finish the book you want to call him up and talk about it.

Listen, I've got a tip for you. Don't do it. Years ago I wrote a book and dais how sometimes I wanted to call the author in the middle of the night, and this guy named Ottinger had his name down as author, and so many weird kids called him up in the middle of the night that the poor guy lost it. He went up to Maine or Vermont and quit writing and only leaves his house once a year. He always sees his shadow, and it's always six more weeks of winter.

I wouldn't want that to happen to Chip Harrison.

I've already read the rest of the books, and I know that Chip went to work for Leo Haig and takes care of tropical fish when he's not helping Haig solve crimes. If you haven't read those books, go out and get them right now. Instead of wasting your time reading this crap I have to write.

Anyway, I like old Chip. I think Phoebe would like him, too. And I hope you liked him, but if you didn't, well, tough. What do you expect me to do about it, anyway?

Oh, yeah. The business about the name. Lawrence Block is now listed as the author of the Chip Harrison books, They had Chip's name as author originally, but now they're supposed to be by this Lawrence Block. Same as my book is supposed to be by old Ottinger.

Well, I don't have to believe that if I don't want to. And neither do you.

That's what Hilton Crofield has to say, and I wouldn't attempt to improve on it. If you've enjoyed *No Score,* you'll very likely have a good time with *Chip Harrison Scores Again,* and may then wend your way through *Make Out With Murder* and *The Topless Tulip Caper.* If you didn't much care for *No Score,* well, you probably won't like the other, either. But I don't want to talk you out of anything. Best to buy them anyway, just to be on the safe side.

I thought it might prove difficult to write a sequel to *No Score,* but in several respects *Chip Harrison Scores Again* is probably a better book. Some of the characters, especially Geraldine, the South Carolina madam, seem to me more interesting and better realized than those in the first book, and I kind of like the story's arc. And, if it's still boyish, it's also bittersweet. I like bittersweet.

Then in 1996, Signet reissued all four of the Chip Harrison titles as paperbacks, and had the devil of a time packaging them. They wanted to call them mysteries, and the third and fourth books, *Make Out With Murder* and *The Topless Tulip Caper*, were certainly that, private-eye puzzle mysteries, although not without the dash of levity and erotica that makes Chip Chip. But *No Score* and *Scores Again* aren't crime novels by any stretch of the imagination. "It is a mystery" the back cover of *No Score* shouts, not once but three times. But it's *not* a mystery, no matter how many times they say it is.

But the next one is. . . .

MAKE OUT WITH MURDER

Chip Harrison is several things.

First, he's the narrator and protagonist of four novels: *No Score, Chip Harrison Scores Again, Make Out With Murder,* and *The Topless Tulip Caper.*

Secondly, he's the credited author of those books, or was in their first appearance; more recently they've been republished in various editions as by Lawrence Block.

And he's also the series character in a series with an identity crisis. Because the first two books are lighthearted sexy novels of a young man's coming of age, while the third and fourth are deductive mystery novels. (They're also lighthearted and sexy.)

Here's what happened: Sometime in the late 1960s, while I was still living in New Brunswick, New Jersey, I wrote a book I called "The Lecher in the Rye". The title says it all; it was a Salingeresque romp about a youth's efforts to acquire sexual experience. A couple of publishers almost bought it, and then one did—Knox Burger, at Gold Medal Books. Knox had bought several books from me over the years, but I don't believe he knew at the time who Chip Harrison was. What did he care? He liked the book, improved the title to *No Score,* commissioned a great piece of cover art, and sent the book out into the world, where it did remarkably well, going into two or three printings.

It did well enough so that Gold Medal might have asked for a sequel, but it didn't occur to anyone there. It occurred to me, though, because I really enjoyed writing in Chip's voice, and thought it might be interesting to see what he did next. By the time I wrote it my wife and kids and I had moved to a farm a mile from the Delaware River, where I found it impossible to get any work done. I took an apartment on West Thirty-fifth Street and wrote several books there over a period of a year or so. One of them was *Chip Harrison Scores Again.* (I don't remember what I called it, but it wasn't that.)

I had fun with the book, and Gold Medal was happy with it. Knox Burger had left to set up shop as an agent—some years later I'd become one of his clients—and Walter Fultz took over, and enlisted the same artist to do the cover. But she worked from models, and the model she'd used before was too old for the role, and the guy she picked to replace him was far too tall and worldly to be Chip. It was the cover of *No Score* that had drawn all those young female readers, and the sequel didn't sell nearly as well.

Oh well.

A few years later my marriage was over and I was living by myself on West Fifty-eighth Street, around the corner from what would soon become Matthew Scudder's hotel. And I remembered how

I'd enjoyed writing as and of Chip Harrison, but how could he go on coming of age? One bildungsroman per character is generally enough. Two is really pushing it. Three is out of the question.

And how could I let him get older? His youth and naïveté were part of his charm. Without them he was just a gnarly guy who didn't get laid as much as he'd have liked to, and if I wanted that all I had to do was look in the mirror.

But suppose he went to work for a private detective. And suppose the guy was a poor man's Nero Wolfe, a sort of road company Nero Wolfe. Suppose he was a great reader of mysteries who idolized Nero Wolfe and—yes!—believed that Wolfe really existed, and that he might someday so distinguish himself as to be invited to dine at Wolfe's table.

And Chip, who had presumably actually written *No Score* and its sequel, would be hired not merely to play Archie Goodwin to this fellow, but to write up the cases and publish them.

Worked like a charm. And it allowed Chip to remain the same age forever, because that's what fictional private eyes do. They remain forever young. There's a passage somewhere—it may be in one of the two Chip Harrison stories—in which Leo Haig tells young Chip to be grateful for his profession, as it's as good as a dip in Ponce de Leon's fountain.

Or words to that effect.

I called the first Chip Harrison mystery *The Cornish Chicks Score*. Gold Medal seemed to like having "score" in the title, and that would do it. And the five sisters were of Cornish descent, and the title would play on the Cornish game hen, that fancy chicken Victor Borge was raising for the American dinner table.

So they called it *Make Out With Murder*. Well, okay. Then

a few years later Alison & Busby, a UK firm, brought out a hardcover edition and called it *Five Little Rich Girls*. That's a whole batch of titles, and I can't say I'm crazy about any of them, but it's been *Make Out With Murder* more often than not, so that's the name it will continue to bear in its new life as an ebook.

Ah well. I'm older than I was when I began writing as and about Chip, and in all likelihood, Dear Reader, so are you. Almost everybody is.

But not Chip. He hasn't aged a day.

THE TOPLESS TULIP SCORE

By now Walter Fultz had moved on, and Joe Elder, whom I'd known back in the Scott Meredith days, was Chip's editor. At some point after he'd agreed to publish *Make Out With Murder*, I went in to meet Joe, who hadn't known who was lurking behind Chip Harrison's name.

He agreed that a fourth book would work out all right, and I went home to write it. I'd already made Haig an avid aquarist, with tropical fish serving him as orchids served Nero Wolfe. And, happily enough, I knew something about tropical fish.

When I delivered the book Joe had a complaint I'd rarely heard in many years in the world of paperback fiction.

"There's not enough sex," he said.

In response, I went through the book page by page until I could find a place where I could wedge in a sex scene. And Chip, after recounting it in some detail, apologizes for it as having not much to do with the book; he explains that his editor, Joe Elder, insisted he augment the book's sexual content. So, although the incident really did take place, Chip thinks it's gratitutious, and rather hopes Mr. Elder will change his mind and take it out again.

The title was easy. A topless dancer named Tulip? Well, how's *The Topless Tulip Score?* That keeps the *score* motif, which sort of got lost in Book Three.

And stayed lost. The title, as you can see, wound up as *The Topless Tulip Caper.* Which I like better, truth to tell.

Ah, Jesus, these books were fun to write. I can only hope they're still fun to read.

BERNIE RHODENBARR SERIES

In 1999, twenty years after its initial publication, Mystery Guild chose to bring out a special leather-bound edition of the third Bernie Rhodenbarr book, *The Burglar who Liked to Quote Kipling.* I wrote the following as an introduction for the volume, and indeed for the whole series:

In the spring of 1976 I was living in Hollywood, in an establishment called the Magic Hotel. It was named for, and loosely affiliated with, the Magic Castle, a club for magicians that was something of a local institution. The hotel itself consisted of spacious one-bedroom apartments, occupied in the main by New York actors with short-term work in Los Angeles. The place was clean and well managed, the rent was remarkably reasonable, and I was very lucky to be there.

Nothing else in my life was going all that well. Someone, probably H. L. Mencken, once suggested that the hand of God had taken hold of the country by the state of Maine and lifted, so that everything loose wound up in southern California. That's more or less how I'd got there, in a rusted out Ford wagon, taking nine months and change to make the trip from New York. I was, you must understand, in no particular hurry, since I didn't really believe things would be any better there than they'd been in New York.

I was going through a bad patch, the details of which need not concern us here. Suffice it to say that my life wasn't working very well, and my career had ground to a halt. I wrote a few books that no one wanted to publish, and when I tried to write more, I couldn't get very far. Sixty pages into a novel, I'd be unable to think of a reason for any of the characters to go on with it.

Writing, unfortunately, was the only work I'd done for the past fifteen years, and the only thing I was at all qualified for. So I couldn't figure out what to do, and reading the employment classifieds just filled me with despair. *Man wanted to sweep up after the horses.* Hmmm, that sounds like something I might be able to do. *Experience a must.* No, never mind. Forget it.

And then one day a little voice said, "Don't rule out crime."

Let me interrupt this with a question. Are you sure you want to read this? Not the book, you're going to love the book. But this introduction. Like, what's the point?

I mean, it's not as though this is a book you have to read for class, or for a Great Books discussion group. Like its author, it's still too young to be a venerable classic, something that might require an introduction to place it in its historical context, or somehow make it a little easier for you to make head or tail out of it. The books I write aren't hard to read. If there's one thing they are it's accessible. They need an introduction about as much as Bernie needs a key to the front door.

This particular volume, handsomely printed and bound, may well hold up long enough to be read by another generation of readers, and, if present trends continue, the youngsters might need a little help working out the intricacies of anything written in complete sentences. An introduction might indeed serve them, if somebody can be found to explain it to them. But what has that got to do with you, Gentle Reader, living happily in the here and now?

You can read this book without assistance. As a matter of fact, there's a fair chance you've already read it. Perhaps you've bought this splendid edition because you wanted to upgrade from that ratty paperback copy before it falls apart altogether. Perhaps you once owned the book but made the common mistake of lending it out. You knew your friend would like it, and the scoundrel proved you right by liking it too much to return it. Well, you've replaced it at last, and you won't make the mistake of lending *this* copy, will you?

Are you beginning to get the point? Why are you wasting your time on this twaddle when you could be reading the book? Ready to fast forward? No?

Oh, all right. Let's get on with it, then. . .

"Don't rule out crime," the voice said.

Ridiculous, I thought. Commit a crime and the world is made of glass, and a person could cut himself. What did I know about committing crimes?

"Experience is not a requirement," the voice countered. "Show somebody a gun, he doesn't ask to see your résumé."

Suppose I got arrested?

"It might be unpleasant," the voice allowed. "On the other hand, matters like food and clothing and shelter would no longer be a problem."

Hmmm, I thought.

But what kind of a criminal might I be? I at once ruled out anything that might put me on the receiving or inflicting end of violence. In fact, I would have to avoid any sort of confrontation. Embezzlement was not without appeal, but you had to have a job first.

Burglary, I thought, and the more I thought the more I liked it. It seemed somehow akin to writing—you set your own hours, you avoided human contact, and, if you were successful, you managed to touch the lives of people you never even met.

I began practicing, teaching myself to slip the lock of my hotel room with a credit card which, alas, had long since ceased to have any other practical application. This proved handy one evening when I forgot my key, or would have, but for my having forgotten my credit card as well. I picked up a spare key at the desk and went to bed.

How far might I have gone with this? Hard to say. One afternoon, thinking about it, I wondered what I would do if the cops walked in on me in the middle of a burglary. I decided that, with a hitherto unblemished record, I'd probably get probation and return to the straight and narrow. And suppose, my writer's mind suggested, just suppose I surrendered, ready to cop a plea, and the police found a dead body in the next room. Then what?

That would be a problem, I thought.

A problem? Hell, that would be a *book*.

And over the next several weeks I wrote the opening chapters of *Burglars Can't Be Choosers*.

I didn't intend for it to come out funny. Remember, I got the idea by imagining myself in the very fix Bernie finds himself in as the book opens, arrested for burglary with a murder victim in the next room. If there was anything intrinsically amusing in the situation, I couldn't see it.

But Bernie emerged, attitude in place, as I wrote the opening pages. This is coming out funny, I thought, more than a little perturbed. Instead of trying to fix it, I let it be what it wanted to be.

And Bernie saved me from a life of crime. Lee Wright at Random House read the opening chapters and struck a deal with my agent, and I finished the book and decided it was better than stealing.

I never expected I would write more than that single book about my buttoned-down burglar. But in the months following the first book's completion, I found him very much on my mind. I had enjoyed being that character during the writing of the book, seeing the world through his eyes, speaking in his distinctive voice. I had set the book in New York—even from three thousand miles away it never occurred to me to set it anywhere else—and now I was living in New York once more, and I'd just finished slogging away to little purpose at a World War II novel, and why not write something I'd enjoy?

Random House published *The Burglar in the Closet*, and I seemed to be writing a series.

Well, almost. The way I see it, the Burglar books really became a series with the book you'll be able to read in a moment, as soon as we get this tedious introduction out of the way. *The Burglar Who Liked to Quote Kipling*—with this book, Bernie truly realized himself as a series character.

Let me explain that. The character never really changed. I somehow knew who Bernie was from the moment he stepped on stage in the first book. But it was in *Kipling* that he got himself a life.

In the preceding books he has a few aspects of a life. He has an apartment, he has some friends and neighbors, he has a dentist, he has a friendly enemy in the person of Ray Kirschmann. But in the third book of the series he acquires the shop, Barnegat Books, and becomes not merely a burglar but an antiquarian bookseller as well. And, two doors down the street, he finds a best friend in the small person of Carolyn Kaiser, lesbian poodle-groomer. (The phrase, I should point out, can be confusing. Carolyn is a lesbian who grooms poodles, not a groomer of lesbian poodles.)

In *The Burglar Who Liked to Quote Kipling*, Bernie's world is fully realized. Other supporting players will turn up from time to time, and the action moves all over New York's five boroughs—and even makes a brief foray out of the city in *The Burglar in the Library*. But the basic dynamic never has to change.

The book received the first-ever Nero Wolfe Award, citing it as the best mystery of the year. I don't know that it's stronger or weaker than other books in the series, but I've always been pleased that it was the won to win the award, because of the way it set things up for the books that followed. If the Burglar books were a TV series, *Kipling* would be the pilot.

Five books in, Bernie went into a sort of suspended animation. *The Burglar Who Painted Like Mondrian* was well received, and I certainly wanted to write more books about Bernie, but it began to look as though it wasn't going to happen. I made some brief attempts that aborted after twenty or thirty pages, and time passed, and Book #6 began to seem less and less likely.

But I kept thinking about Bernie and Carolyn. And, after an eleven-year gap, I went off to San Francisco, holed up in a Tenderloin hotel, and wrote *The Burglar Who Traded Ted Williams*. And the books have come along every year or so ever since.

During the drought, I got the same question every time I made a public appearance. *When are you gonna write another book about Bernie?* Or, *Are you ever gonna write another book about Bernie?*

Finally, in a bookshop in Scottsdale, Arizona, I was able to answer that questions as I'd longed to answer it. A sixth Burglar book was written, I informed the two nice ladies who'd inquired so plaintively. Moreover, it was scheduled for publication, and would be out in a matter of months.

They couldn't have been happier, and did everything but dance. Then their faces fell. Would this jubilation hurt the feelings of Matthew Scudder, my other series character? Might he take it amiss that they were making such a fuss over Bernie Rhodenbarr?

"Please," the begged, "don't misunderstand. We absolutely love Matt. But we want to marry Bernie."

* * *

MATTHEW SCUDDER SERIES

Eight Million Ways to Die, my fifth novel about Matthew Scudder, was published in 1982. Many years and many books later, my publishers at William Morrow determined that a new hardcover edition of the book would find a ready market in libraries, and perhaps with collectors as well. I pointed out that it was indeed a good year for it, that 2007 marked the book's twenty-fifth anniversary. And so they put some muscle into the book, and sold an encouraging number of copies, and I got into the spirit of things and contributed an afterword, which appears here:

> I started writing about Matthew Scudder sometime in late 1973. My other series have been unintentional—I began by writing a single book (or, in the case of Keller, a single short story) and one thing led to another. With Scudder, however, I knew before I wrote the first chapter of the first book that I was hatching a series. I wrote a proposal, and when Bill Grose at Dell approved it, I wrote the first three books (*The Sins of the Fathers, Time to Murder and Create,* and *In the Midst of Death*) one after the other.
>
> Dell published them in 1975–6, and that wasn't a particularly good time to be publishing original fiction with Dell. While the books got a decent critical reception, with the second volume shortlisted for an Edgar Allan Poe award, the books were not effectively distributed and did not sell well. I figured that was the end of Matthew Scudder, but I was mistaken, and, as it was to turn out, not for the last time.
>
> I wrote a pair of Scudder novelettes, "Out the Window"

and "A Candle for the Bag Lady," both published in *Alfred Hitchcock's Mystery Magazine*, and then in 1980 I wrote the fourth Scudder novel, *A Stab in the Dark*. I had no reason to think any publisher would be eager to pick up a failed series, but it was what I wanted to write, and so I wrote it. The first publisher to see it was Don Fine at Arbor House, and he brought it out in hardcover (the Dell editions were paperback originals) and got a nice book club sale, a paperback reprint deal, and some respectful reviews. Matt Scudder was back in business.

But he had begun to change.

That was never part of the agenda back in 1973. I figured Scudder, like almost all characters in genre fiction, would remain essentially the same for as long as I wrote about him. He wouldn't age, nor would he alter his behavior. He'd keep his seat at that back table in Jimmy Armstrong's saloon, and he'd drink his whiskey neat or stir it into his coffee, depending on the hour or his mood or the phase of the moon. For heaven's sake, why should he change?

I'm not sure he had much choice.

I wouldn't presume to argue that the quality of a series is contingent upon the change and growth and aging of the lead character. Much of the appeal of a series lies in the fact that one can return to a world one has previously visited with pleasure, renewing one's acquaintance with characters of whom one has already become fond. I've been chronicling the adventures of Bernie Rhodenbarr for just about as long as I've been writing about Scudder, and Bernie hasn't lost a step or aged a day or gained the slightest shred of self-awareness. And why should he?

With Scudder, I was operating at a different level of realism. I could not take the books as seriously as I needed to if I didn't allow their hero to be affected in one book by the experiences he'd endured in the previous one. He had to grow, he had to change, and he had to age.

This first became evident in *A Stab in the Dark*, which concludes with Scudder getting the first glimmer that his drinking is problematic. He actually walks into an AA meeting—and walks out in a hurry, heading for Armstrong's.

But I had the feeling he'd be back.

Eight Million Ways to Die was the next book, and it wound up twice as long as any of the four earlier volumes. That came about because the book was doing three things at once.

First of all, it was what each of its predecessors had been—a story about the investigation of a crime. That was certainly the main thrust of the narrative, as it ought to be in any piece of crime fiction.

But that was only part of it. Even as he attempts to solve Kim Dakkinen's murder, Scudder struggles with his own alcoholism, which has reached crisis proportions. His efforts to remain sober, and his reluctant exploration of Alcoholics Anonymous, constitute a major element in the story.

Finally, as the title would suggest, the book is a meditation on the perilous nature of life in New York—and, indeed, of human life anywhere.

I wrote the book in the fall of 1981, having recently returned from a summer spent knocking around the country by Greyhound bus. I was now living on Haven Avenue, in Washington Heights, although my life was still largely centered in Greenwich Village, where I'd resided prior to my bus trip.

Most days, once I'd finished writing, I'd pick up a copy of the *Daily News* and take the A train downtown. On the train, I'd still be very much in Scudder's world, and the stories I'd read— of random violence and sudden death—would often find their way into the next day's writing.

Writing the book, I was concerned about its length. It was clearly going to be long for a crime novel, especially long for a first-person detective story. But I knew I had to give the book its head, and I didn't try to hold it back. Nor, I must say, did I get any grief on the subject from either my editor, Arnold Ehrlich, nor my publisher, Don Fine. On the contrary, they hurried the book into production—Arbor House almost always hurried things along those days, like Patton outrunning his supply lines—and it was published in the early summer of 1982, just twenty-five years ago as I write these lines.

Sheesh. Where did the time go?

Eight Million Ways to Die was a critical success, with a very strong review in the *New York Times*. A photographer from *Time* came to my apartment in Greenpoint—perhaps inspired by Scudder's client, Chance, I'd moved there shortly after completing the novel—to take my picture, but neither it nor the magazine's review ever ran. Even so, the book sold reasonably well, with a small second printing and a book club edition. It was shortlisted for an Edgar and won the Shamus award outright, and brought the whole Scudder series more attention than it had previously received.

And I figured the series was over.

God knows that wasn't what I wanted. I liked Matthew Scudder, and found his personality of unceasing interest and his voice an engaging one in which to write. But it seemed to me that his story was told.

Each of the five books in the series was a novel in its own right. But one could also view the Scudder oeuvre as a five-part novel, its conclusion reached in the final volume. By its end Scudder has undergone a catharsis, and there's generally a one-to-a-customer limit on catharses, in fiction if not in real life. Matthew Scudder had just contended with and apparently solved the central problem of his existence. He might have a life after so doing, indeed he could hardly continue to have a life otherwise, but was it a life anyone would need to read about? More to the point, was it one I'd have any call to write about?

Scudder's *d'etre*, I was wont to tell people, had lost its *raison*. And that seemed all too evident when I made attempts at a sixth book and watched them flatten out and die on the page.

There was no help for it. I was done with him.

Well, obviously, I was wrong. There have been eleven Matthew Scudder novels since then, with *All the Flowers Are Dying* the most recent. The man has continued to grow and change and age. In the eighth book, a killer from their shared past brought him together with Elaine Mardell, and romance bloomed. A few books down the line they got married and moved across the street to the Parc Vendome. Somewhere along the line Scudder acquired a private investigator's license, and shortly thereafter he gave it up.

And now, as it happens, I find myself once again fairly certain that Scudder and I are done with each other. The man is in his late sixties; while his health remains good, he's a little old to go on having these adventures. He seems ready for retirement.

Still, I've been wrong before. One never knows.

* * *

I should probably say something about the movie. I get questions about it all the time. People read books, but they want to talk about movies. Who knows why?

Oliver Stone optioned the book and wrote one or two confusing drafts of the screenplay. Then other hands took over, and the picture limped along to completion; it was released in 1986, got negative reviews, did little business, and that was that. Jeff Bridges and Andy Garcia did excellent work in the film, but that wasn't enough to save it, and the people in charge took final cut away from director Hal Ashby; since his greatest strength was in the cutting room, this didn't help. (It was Ashby's last film, and I don't know that it hastened his premature death, but I wouldn't be surprised. When I met him on the set I noticed a sweet sadness about him, and when I saw the movie I had an idea where it came from.)

The picture didn't have much to do with the book—it was set in Los Angeles, an odd choice for this thoroughly New York story—but I've never felt that the primary aim of a filmmaker ought to be to bring an author's vision to the screen. The object, it seems to me, must be to make a good movie. Which, alas, didn't happen.

I couldn't be more pleased to have *Eight Million Ways to Die* available again in a handsome hardcover edition, a full quarter of a century after its original appearance. The Arbor House first edition has become highly collectible—a curious word, that, which would appear to mean simply that people are happy to pay more for it than it really ought to be worth—and even copies of the second printing and the book club edition command a substantial premium. This new edition will allow collectors, as well as enthusiasts who just want a well-bound permanent copy for their shelves, to fill a longstanding gap.

And it will also allow libraries to restock a book that appears on a lot of lists of classic crime fiction. I'm delighted, and I hope you've enjoyed it.

EVAN TANNER SERIES

A few years ago HarperCollins arranged to acquire the rights to my eight novels about Evan Tanner, and reissued them as mass-market paperbacks. I agreed to provide an afterword for each volume, and have reproduced them here. Some material was repeated in each afterword, but through judicious editing I've spared you that. . .

Evan Michael Tanner was conceived in the summer of 1956, in New York's Washington Square Park. But his gestation period ran to a decade.

That summer was my first stay in New York, and what a wonder it was. After a year at Antioch College, I was spending three months in the mailroom at Pines Publications, as part of the school's work-study program. I shared an apartment on Barrow Street with a couple of other students, and I spent all my time—except for the forty weekly hours my job claimed—hanging out in the Village. Every Sunday afternoon I went to Washington Square, where a couple of hundred people gathered to sing folk songs around the fountain. I spent evenings in coffeehouses, or at somebody's apartment.

What an astonishing variety of people I met! Back home in Buffalo, people had run the gamut from A to B. (The ones I knew, that is. Buffalo, I found out later, was a pretty rich human landscape, but I didn't have a clue at the time.)

But in the Village I met socialists and monarchists and Welsh nationalists and Catholic anarchists and, oh, no end of exotics. I met people who worked and people who found other ways of making a living, some of them legal. And I soaked all this up for three months and went back to school, and a year later I started selling stories and dropped out of college to take a job at a literary agency. Then I went back to school and then I dropped out again, and ever since I've been writing books, which is to say I've found a legal way of making a living without working.

Where's Tanner in all this?

Hovering, I suspect, somewhere on the edge of thought. And then in 1962 I was back in Buffalo with a wife and a daughter and another daughter on the way, and two facts, apparently unrelated, came to my attention one right after the other.

Fact One: it is apparently possible for certain rare individuals to live without sleep.

Fact Two: Two hundred fifty years after the death of Queen Anne, the last reigning monarch of the House of Stuart, there was still (in the unlikely person of a German princeling) a Stuart pretender to the English throne.

I picked up the first fact in an article on sleep in *Time Magazine*, the second while browsing the Encyclopedia Britannica. They seemed to go together, and I found myself thinking of a character whose sleep center had been destroyed, and who consequently had an extra eight hours in the day to contend with. What would he do with the extra time? Well, he could learn languages. And what passion would drive him? Why, he'd be plotting and scheming to oust Betty Battenberg, the Hanoverian usurper, and restore the Stuarts to their rightful place on the throne of England.

I put the idea on the back burner, and then I must have

unplugged the stove, because it was a couple of more years before Tanner was ready to be born. By then a Stuart restoration was just one of his disparate passions. He was to be a champion of lost causes and irredentist movements, and I was to write eight books about him.

The Thief Who Couldn't Sleep was Tanner's debut, and it might never have happened if I hadn't brought home a dinner guest one evening in 1965. The fellow's name was Lincoln W. Higgie—Bill to his friends—and he'd recently returned from Turkey, where he'd spent a couple of years earning a precarious living smuggling rare coins and antiquities out of the country. (Precarious because it was illegal; if the authorities caught you they might sentence you to death, which was bad, or throw you into prison, which was demonstrably worse.)

Bill Higgie was a numismatist—if you Google him, you'll find he wrote a book on the coinage, tokens, and paper money of the Virgin Islands—and I was editing a numismatic magazine at the time. He showed up at the office, I brought him home to dinner, he brought a bottle of Bushmill's as a hostess gift, we sat up late and drank it, and he told me a story of a horde of gold coins hidden in a house in Balekesir, and of the too—late efforts of a couple of free spirits from Aramco to recover it.

Remarkably, I recalled our conversation the next day. And, more remarkably, I remembered the as-yet unemployed fellow with the damaged sleep center and the passion for lost causes. I put the two together and, well, I hope you've enjoyed the result.

Tanner was my first series character, but I didn't know that when I started writing about him. As pleased as I was with

The Thief Who Couldn't Sleep, he wasn't yet a series character because you can't have a one-book series. (Or at least that's what I thought at the time. Some years later I wrote a book called *The Specialists*, and it did in fact turn out to be a one-book series. But I digress. . .)

By the time I finished *Thief*, I knew I wanted to write more about this guy. I'd written several novels under my own name by then, plus several dozen under pen names, but it seemed to me that this was the first book with a voice that was uniquely mine. That felt good, and I wanted more of it.

Thief ends with Tanner the putative employee of a government agency so secret that he doesn't know its name, and his boss doesn't know that Tanner doesn't really work for him. So his boss sends him off to rescue a particularly odious Nazi war criminal, and Tanner accepts the assignment, and carries it out in his own idiosyncratic way.

What a different place the world was when I wrote this book! There was barely a patch of rust on the Iron Curtain; not only were perestroika and glasnost decades in the future, but the world still had some turning to do before the Prague Spring of 1968. The Iron Curtain's gone, the Soviet Union's gone, and Czechoslovakia has bifurcated itself amoeba-style into the Czech Republic and Slovakia, the last a development no one anticipated but which Tanner (like an abiding majority of Czechs and Slovaks) would have wholeheartedly approved.

Kotacek, the unpleasant chap Tanner rescues, is of course a Slovak, not a Czech, but somehow the notion of calling the book *The Canceled Slovak* never entered my mind. Go figure.

I don't know if there was a Latvian Army-in-Exile back in the Sixties.

What I do know (or thought I knew) is that there was a *Lithuanian* Army-in-Exile. It came to my attention sometime in the late 1950s, when I was sitting around with a group of people that included Dave Van Ronk and Tom Condit, and someone (Dave? Tom? someone else?) mentioned a friend or acquaintance who'd found a particularly efficacious way to avoid getting drafted. (We were all preoccupied with avoiding the draft, as if it would cause the flu. It's hard to remember why. I don't know that the Army would have had me, and if it had, serving would very likely have done me no harm, and might even have done me some good. That's hindsight talking, of course; at the time, I dreaded the prospect.)

And how had this worthy escaped military service? Had he (like another legendary genius) smeared himself with filth and reported for his pre-induction physical reeking, only to be summarily dismissed and written off as an ambulatory psychotic? Had he (like other mythical beings) made a strong physical pass at the consulting psychiatrist? Had he cultivated a psychopathic stare and demanded to be given a gun so he could kill the filthy Russians? (And would that really work, or would they just give him a big hug and send him to Officer Candidate School?)

No, he had accepted a commission as an officer in the Lithuanian Army-in-Exile.

"That'll do it," someone pointed out. "If you enter into the service of a foreign power, they can't take you into the U.S. armed forces. Of course, you get stripped of your citizenship."

That seemed extreme. Suppose one wanted to run for president one day? Which seemed a stretch, admittedly, but still, one did want to keep one's options open. Still, the idea of

marching and saluting and drilling in the Catskills with a batch
of Lithuanian patriots had a certain appeal.

And it evidently lingered, because it came to mind when it
was time to write a third book about Evan Michael Tanner; if
there truly was a Lithuanian Army-in-Exile, Tanner would have
to be a part of it. I'm not sure what prompted me to change
the Lithuanians to Latvians. In time I would meet a Latvian
painter in New Brunswick, New Jersey, Valdi Maris by name,
and some years after that I would have a Latvian girlfriend,
Zane Berzins by name, and now, years later, I am still able to say
Happy New Year in Latvian, though I'll admit I don't get much
call for it. But back then all I knew about Latvia was that it was
sandwiched in between Lithuania and Estonia.

What I liked about the story was the notion of Tanner
embarking on a harebrained mission to bring one person out
from behind the Iron Curtain and accumulating an increasing
menagerie along the way. It was, as you might imagine, fun to
write—but what you might not imagine is the way my whole
world changed while I was writing it.

Because I started out writing it in New Jersey, where I was
living. And then I got involved in a mad affair, overflowing
with drink and drama, and I wound up running away from
everybody. I got on a plane at Idlewild and got off it in Dublin,
and I entered the Republic of Ireland with an extra pair of
underwear, an extra pair of socks, and the partial manuscript
of Tanner #3. I had, as Oscar Wilde put it, nothing to declare
but my genius, and I wasn't so sure about that, either.

I took a room in a tatty bed-and-breakfast on the north
side of Dublin, in Amiens Street, and I rented a typewriter in
a shop around the corner in Talbot Street, and I bought some
typing paper that was about an inch longer and a half-inch

narrower than what I was used to, and within the month I'd finished the book.

I think I had about a third of it written when I was interrupted by life, but I can't be sure, because when I go back and re-read it, I can't find the break. My life before and after could hardly have changed more, but the book's life was somehow uninterrupted. Tanner, it seemed, really didn't care what I was going through. He had problems of his own.

I should add that there was a stationer in O'Connell Street called Eaton's, and that it was there that I came upon a book called *Teach Yourself Latvian*. That sounded more like an inventive schoolboy's curse than a book anyone would want to buy, but I bought it, by George, and that accounts for the Latvian phrases you'll find in these pages. I can't swear they're accurate, but really, what do you care?

About the title: after the general enthusiasm for *The Canceled Czech*, I wanted a comparable title for the third book. I came up with a few, including *The Lettish Tomatoes*, which I rather like, but the publisher chose *Tanner's Twelve Swingers*. Which I flat hated. I've restored other titles, but I think I'll leave this one alone. For the time being, anyway.

If you've been picking up these splendid new editions of the Tanner books as they appear, and if you've been reading not only the books themselves but these self-indulgent afterwords of mine, and if (finally) you've the sort of old-trunk-in-the-attic memory that retains trivial information, then you may recall that the book immediately preceding this one, *Tanner's Twelve Swingers*, was begun in New Brunswick, New Jersey, and completed in Dublin.

When it was finished, I sent it off to my agent and returned the typewriter to the firm around the corner from whom I'd rented it. I'd landed in Dublin in mid-January, and it was the middle of February when I set out to see the country.

I'd been to Ireland once before, and had felt a strong immediate connection to the country. I thought I might like to live there, and knew that one thing I didn't want to do, not for a while, was go back to the States. So I bundled up my things and hit the road.

I didn't have all that much to bundle up, having arrived with a change of socks and underwear and a manuscript. But of course I'd bought some clothing since I'd arrived, so I purchased a knapsack and took a bus south of Dublin to a town called Bray. From there I figured I could hitchhike.

But that turned out to be uncommonly difficult. I eventually learned that just a week or two earlier a hitchhiker had pulled a knife on a man, forcing his benefactor to drive miles out of his way before releasing him unharmed. Now back home, if this got any coverage at all, the headline would have been something along the lines of "Kindly Hitchhiker Spares Moron's Life." But in Ireland, where this sort of thing didn't happen, it was a nine-days wonder, and people who'd always picked up hitchhikers without a second thought now kept their eyes fixed straight ahead and drove on by.

It took a while, but I managed to hitchhike to Arklow. I think that's where I bought the bike, but it may have been further along, in Wexford Town. It seemed like a good idea at the time, but it turned out to be anything but.

For two reasons, really. One was that I was in very hilly terrain, and that I was always going downhill on a bike that was careening out of control or walking alongside the bike as I pushed it up a hill.

In the rain.

I kept at it, and I got as far as a town called Enniscorthy. I knew the town from a ballad of the 1798 Rising. I put up at a bed and breakfast run by a Mrs. Twomey, whose young son greatly admired the bicycle. I tried with all the guile of a New Yorker to sell that bicycle to Mrs. Twomey, and she, innocent denizen of rural Ireland, just bided her time while the price dropped. After I'd been there three days—a long time to be in Enniscorthy, unless Father Murphy's leading you in battle against the yeomen—I offered to give Mrs. Twomey the bike in exchange for what I owed her for my bed and breakfast. She decided that would be all right, and I hoisted my knapsack and got out of there, and by then, of course, all Ireland had forgotten about the villainous hitchhiker, and I had no trouble getting rides—to Cork City, and then on to Bantry.

In Bantry, in the Anchor Hotel, I bought an Olivetti portable typewriter and began writing *The Scoreless Thai*. I wrote three or four chapters, and by then it was the middle of March, and something made me decide to return to the life I'd left behind in the States. I hitchhiked to Shannon and flew home, and when I'd landed I got back to work and wrote the rest of the book.

Tanner's previous adventures all took place in Europe. Something about the character seemed to lend itself to border-hopping around the crazy quilt of Eastern Europe, and I wasn't sure how well Tanner's particular skills would lend themselves to an Asian landscape. I guess it worked out okay.

I thought of the title early on, and found it irresistible, even inevitable. A story about a Siamese who couldn't get laid? I mean, what else could you possibly call it?

Some witling at Fawcett promptly changed it to *Two For Tanner*. I can't begin to guess why, anymore than I can tell you who the titular two were supposed to be. Sheesh. *The Scoreless Thai,* that's the title, now and forever.

Lost causes?

Don't count on it.

One thing that's become evident to me, in the course of chronicling the adventures of Evan Michael Tanner, is that no cause is ever truly lost. They may not be steaming, but that doesn't mean they're not sitting patiently on a back burner, simmering away.

For instance. . .

In his first appearance, *The Thief Who Couldn't Sleep,* Tanner is sheltered in Ireland by his fellow members of the Irish Republican Army, an organization which at the time surely appeared to amount to nothing more than a batch of spirited if delusional folk given to ballad-singing and unable to accept the reality of a partition agreement that had been in force for over forty years. Yes, they'd made some noise over the decades, and chucked a few bombs, but the Troubles were surely a thing of the past, were they not?

Well, no, they weren't. Within five years of that book's publication, I had the curious experience of riding through the Bogside in Derry while it was under IRA occupation. Streets were barricaded, and we passed a flat-bed lorry captained by a gaunt fellow wearing a mask; small boys were bringing him empty milk bottles, and he was filling them with petrol. If reclamation of the Six Counties was a lost cause, surely no one had told any of the people we saw that day.

And so on.

Tanner, you'll recall, belonged to the Latvian Army in Exile, as well as groups advocating independence for the various components of Yugoslavia. Fat chance, I thought at the time—

and now the Baltic States are independent, and Yugoslavia has divided itself into six countries. (Or more, if you count Srbska and Kosovo and. . . oh, never mind.)

And so on.

What could be less a hot-button issue than the Armenian genocide of 1915? Tanner, a member of the League for the Restoration of Cilician Armenia, might not see it that way. And neither did the editor in Istanbul who had the temerity to deny the official denial of that holocaust. Nor did the fellow who assassinated him, just days ago as I write these lines.

I could go on in this vein. Causes, lost and found, burn hot one day and cold the next. When I first wrote about Tanner, the idea that they'd ever resume fighting the Thirty Years War in the north of Ireland seemed pretty farfetched. A few years later, the prospect of peace in those counties seemed every bit as remote. And now things have settled down again. For the time being, anyway, though that may change again between the writing of these lines and your reading of them.

Lost causes? I'll tell you, causes don't get lost. They may get misplaced, but sooner or later somebody finds them all over again.

Which brings us to Canada.

Huh? How does it bring us to Canada?

Irony, as you may have noticed, is frequently in the picture in the Tanner books, and Canada seemed to offer it in abundance as a venue for our sleepless hero. It had a vast and utterly porous border with the United States, and all you had to do to cross from one country to another was answer the uniformed dude who asked you where you were born. (*Boo-faw-lo*, said a young friend of mine, in response to a functionary on the Peace Bridge. My friend thought he was being funny. The man thought otherwise, and threatened to haul him out of the car, just to teach him a lesson, but in the end he let us go through, just as they always let everybody go through. Nothing to it.)

Canada boasted a Lost Cause, too, in the advocates of liberation for the francophone province of Quebec. Every once in a while some Quebecois hothead would put a bomb in a mailbox, and a batch of postcards home would get blown to hell, but that was about the extent of it. It was, of course, the sort of cause Tanner would find inspiring, but it wouldn't keep him up nights.

(But he'd be up anyway, wouldn't he? Never mind.)

Irony? Tanner, who leaps international borders the way Superman hops over tall buildings, could find himself refused entry to Canada, so that he'd be the first person who had to sneak in since Wolfe beat Montcalm. (On September 13, 1759, and neither man survived the day—but you knew that, right?) Oh, the possibilities for irony were everywhere, but in the end I set the book in Canada for the same reason that Tanner went there.

I wanted to go to Expo.

He took Minna, but I went by myself—to have a look at it, and to break a longstanding rule and actually know something about the setting of a Tanner book. I spent a week or so in Montreal, and visited the Cuban Pavilion, and I can tell you it's just as described. It was quite remarkable. I don't think they had trapdoors, and I don't for a moment believe they were shanghaiing black people, but I can't absolutely rule it out.

I probably ought to explain about the tiger.

A couple of weeks after I turned in the book, I got a call from my agent. "They want a change," he told me. "They want Arlette to be wearing a tigerskin coat."

"Oh," I said. "Uh, why?"

"So they can call the book *Tanner's Tiger.*"

"They can call it that anyway," I said. They could call anything whatever they wanted, as they'd demonstrated, to my chagrin, with previous books.

"But without the coat," he said, "it wouldn't make any sense."

"It would make as much sense," I pointed out, "as it would for her to be wearing a tigerskin coat." But my heart wasn't in it, and I made the change, modifying it slightly—instead of a coat, I gave her a tigerskin beret, and a tigerskin throw for her bed. It's not a bad title, although I can't say it makes much sense.

You need a passport to cross the Peace Bridge these days, or some lesser form of government-issued photo ID. The world had changed, and that border with it. The Free Quebec movement never got much more violent that the occasional bomb in the occasional post box, though it did achieve some of its goals through peaceful means, and never did find it necessary to blow up the Queen of England.

But here's the thing. You really never do know what the future holds.

Tanner's Virgin, which you've just finished reading (unless you're one of those unaccountable mavericks who read the afterword first), bore a different title when first it saw the light of day back in 1968. I had several editors over the years at Fawcett Gold Medal, including Knox Burger, Walter Fultz, and Joe Elder, but the capo di tutti capi was a man named Ralph Daigh, whom I never met, but who seems to have found a certain satisfaction in changing his authors' titles.

My first book for Fawcett was a noir suspense novel. We were going to call it *Grifter's Game.* I'm not sure what my original working title had been, although I think it may have been *A Little Off the Top;* I know it wasn't *Mona*, which is the title Daigh slapped on it. And why, pray tell? Because he'd recently bought some cover art consisting of a sketch of a woman, so he wanted to call the book by the name of the femme fatale, in order to make the cover appropriate.

The book has since gone through many editions as *Mona* and one as *Sweet Slow Death* (don't ask) and has now finally been reprinted as *Grifter's Game.*

After Daigh changed *The Scoreless Thai* to *Two for Tanner*, I pretty much quit trying to ring the titular bell. I can't swear to it, but I believe the present volume was submitted as *Tanner #6.* When it was published, the title it bore was *Here Comes A Hero.*

Tanner #6 would have been better.

Looking back, it's hard to believe nobody came up with *Tanner's Virgin* back in the day. After all, it was Daigh who'd come up with *Tanner's Tiger* as a title for the book immediately preceding this one. (And had me rewrite a scene so that Tanner's love interest was wearing a tigerskin coat, to justify the title, and so that such a coat could appear on the cover.) *Tanner's Virgin* would seem to be of a piece, so to speak, with *Tanner's Tiger*, and there'd be no rewriting required, as there was already a perfectly good virgin in the book.

Well, nobody thought of it. And if somebody did, would anything have come of it? Probably not, not with *Here Comes A Hero* just crying out to be used.

Sheesh.

* * *

The storylines of Tanner's adventures, as you may have noticed, generally range somewhere between farfetched and absurd. Nevertheless, there's occasionally a grain of genuine grit at the core of Tanner's pearls.

And so it was with *Tanner's Virgin.*

A friend of a friend came back from London with a story. It seems someone asked this rather shady character what had happened to a young woman of their acquaintance. "Well, what do you think happened?" snapped the shady character. "I sold her. I told her that's what would happen, but she would insist on coming along, so I sold her."

Sold her into white slavery, that is to say. In Afghanistan.

And, my source reported, it turned out that this was Mr. Shady's main source of income. He posed as a travel agent, offering fully escorted women-only tours of Afghanistan at an irresistibly low price, and managing to screen out any applicants with close family ties or persons likely to keep tabs on them. Once he had a group of a dozen or so nubile and unattached young women on board, he promptly escorted them to Afghanistan, where he sold the lot of them for whatever the going rate may have been and left them to get on with their lives, or what remained thereof.

"Not a nice person," said the friend of a friend.

So Afghanistan was more or less handed to me. That was a couple of wars ago, and what I knew about the country you could put in a silk ear. Or a sow's purse. Or, less metaphorically, in the Encyclopedia Britannica, which is where I did what I had the temerity to call my research.

Back then, all I knew about Afghanistan was that it was a hippie destination, because it didn't cost much to live there. (It was even cheaper if you'd been sold into white slavery.) I knew about the hippies, and I knew about the coats that some of them (not the ones sold into white slavery) were bringing back, very attractive sheepskin garments with colorful embroidery. And I figured they must have at least one 1955 Chevy there.

Well, that was then and this is now. These days, if you want a 1955 Chevy, you'll have to go to Havana.

The first six Tanner novels, from *The Thief Who Couldn't Sleep* through *Tanner's Virgin* (née *Here Comes a Hero*) were published as mass-market paperback originals by Fawcett Gold Medal. While they were being written and published, I was also publishing hardcover fiction with Macmillan, starting with *Deadly Honeymoon* in 1967. And, when I was ready to write a seventh book about Tanner, I offered it to Macmillan.

Nowadays, almost anyone would assume that the move from paperback original to hardcover was a Big Step Up. And nowadays it generally is. But things were different then, and the most significant reason for Macmillan's publication of *Deadly Honeymoon* was that Gold Medal had already turned it down.

Consider the numbers. Gold Medal paid an advance representing a royalty on the total number of copies *printed*, and generally amounting to somewhere between $2,500 and $3,000. (If they went back for a second printing, they paid a similar advance for all copies printed. This, sad to say, never happened with any of the Tanner books.)

Macmillan's advance was $1,000, against royalties on copies sold, and in return they took 50% of any paperback earnings the book might generate.

Now there were compensations. Macmillan always took me out to lunch. And hardcover books were much more likely to get reviewed, for whatever that's worth. (Not much, I suspect.) And, finally, there was something far more prestigious about hardcover publication. A hardcover book with one's name on it—and perhaps one's photograph on the flap, or even the back cover—looked good on the shelf, and made one's mother proud. It was evidence that one had arrived, even though it might in fact owe its existence to one's having been first rejected by a paperback house.

Me Tanner, You Jane hadn't been rejected by Gold Medal. They seemed perfectly willing to go on publishing Tanner's adventures. The books weren't selling terribly well—as I said, none of the six ever managed to get into a second printing—nor did sales seem to be increasing from one book to the next.

For my own part, I was getting tired of the books—although I'm not sure I was consciously aware of it at the time. For all that the settings changed from book to book, the characters and situations seemed to me to be repetitive. And, annoyingly enough, Tanner wasn't making me rich or famous, and for all that Fawcett was selling upwards of a hundred thousand copies of each title, I never had the sense that anyone out there was actually reading the books, or paying any attention to them.

So my agent and I put our heads together, and one of us—I forget which one—thought perhaps it was time to move Tanner to hard covers, and the other figured it was worth a try. By this time I had an idea and a title, and my agent arranged for me to meet with my editor at Macmillan and pitch it.

My first editor at Macmillan was a woman named Mary Heathcote. She bought and edited *Deadly Honeymoon* and

After the First Death, and moved on before the latter book was published. Her replacement was Alan Rinzler—"I am the new Mary Heathcote," his note to me began—and it was to him that I would propose *Me Tanner, You Jane*.

We'd met before, of course, and had had lunch once or twice. He didn't drink, didn't drink at all, which I found quite remarkable. I thought everyone in publishing drank. I thought it was part of the job description.

Still, he was a bright and personable fellow, and his status as a nondrinker meant there was no great danger in meeting with him in the middle of the afternoon. (CBL read the notation on a good many cards in the Rolodex of one agent I knew; Call Before Lunch was what it stood for.)

So I went in and sat across the desk from him and started talking about this book I planned to write, furnishing him while I was at it with some background on the series, and it didn't seem to be going too well. He looked, dare I say it, hungover.

And his eyes did look to be glazing over, which I've never found to be a good sign. So I talked a little faster, and fabricated some plot elements, and just kept talking, talking, talking, until the poor man held up a hand.

"Stop for a minute," he said. "See, I had some really dynamite hash last night, and I'm not tracking all that well today. But I can see you've got a well thought-out story here, and it sounds good to me, so I'll put through a contract."

So then all I had to do was write the thing.

I don't remember a great deal about the writing of *Me Tanner, You Jane*, and I can't blame it on hash, neither dynamite nor corned beef. I picked the African setting in an effort to make the book different from others in the series, and looked for a dramatic way to get things going. In *The Scoreless Thai*, I'd kicked things off with Tanner locked in a bamboo cage suspended in the air, and awaiting execution; *Me Tanner, You Jane* begins with him already buried.

The opening sequence gave me a chance to use something that had been stuck in my head for a couple of years. While I was living in New Brunswick, New Jersey, I made the acquaintance of a Latvian painter named Valdi Maris. (I had recently published *Tanner's Twelve Swingers,* which involves the Latvian Army in Exile, and a local review of the book had led him to invite me to a party.) His English was good, if accented, but he made an interesting mistake on one word, adding the wrong suffix to a verb form; *comparison* came out *comparisment*.

I really loved that, and I wanted to have a character make errors of that sort, but I never was able to conjure up another example. So one of the chaps involved in Tanner's premature interment says comparisment for comparison. Good, I thought to myself. I've used it, and now I can forget about it.

But evidently I haven't.

Looking back all these years later, it strikes me that having Jane call herself Sheena after the comic book character may be more than happenstance. Because I've long felt that there's a comic-book aspect to this particular novel. (You could perhaps say as much for the whole series, but I think it's truest for MTYJ.) I have a feeling the same thing happened to me when I was writing the book as when I was pitching it to poor Alan Rinzler. I imagined the reader's eyes glazing over, and tried to bring him/her back by making every plot turn a little more outrageous.

I don't dislike the book all these years later, not by any means, but by the time I finished it I knew I was done—not just with the book itself, but with the series. I'm sure I'd have changed my mind if it had been a huge success, or even a rather small success, but all it did was come out and sell a handful of copies and vanish. It didn't even manage to get reprinted in paperback.

What it did do, oddly enough, was remain in print. Nowadays books get remaindered almost before the ink is dry; unless a book continues to sell at a pretty good pace, a publisher drops it from his list and ships the leftover copies to a cut-price wholesaler, and the next thing you know your novel is on the Bargain Books table at Barnes & Noble, pegged at about half the price it command in paperback.

It was not ever thus. Until the government changed the rules, a publisher could keep a book in print as a service to readers and booksellers while still writing off the greater portion of costs for tax purposes. Some swine took the trouble to close this useful loophole, and that was the end of that.

But *Me Tanner, You Jane*, published in 1970, was still available from Macmillan seven or eight years later. I knew this because a copy actually sold, *mirabile dictu*, and I got a royalty check for forty-nine cents. If I'd had any sense—and a few hundred dollars worth of risk capital—I'd have stocked up. I had neither, and all I did was tell Otto Penzler, who promptly stocked up. Shortly thereafter the book disappeared.

And here it is, all these years later, in a handsome paperback edition not that much more expensive than the original Macmillan hardcover.

I do hope you enjoyed it.

The first seven Tanner novels were written and published within a four or five year span. The eighth one took twenty-eight years.

Back in the day, I never made a firm conscious decision to discontinue the series. It felt to me as though I was done with it, and as time passed the likelihood of my ever returning to Tanner grew increasingly remote. There had been reason to stop—the lack of great enthusiasm on the part of readers and publishers, for one thing, and the fact that the stories and characters had seemed to me to be repeating themselves. And it struck me that there was further reason to stay stopped, in that all of the lost causes and irredentist movements to which my sleepless knight belonged had somehow transformed themselves; when I started writing about them they seemed richly comedic, and since then they had turned homicidal.

After Black Sunday, what was even vaguely funny about the IRA and the Irish Troubles? After a few ETA bombings and assassinations, what was amusing about Basque nationalism?

And so on.

It's not unheard of for a writer to stop writing about a series character. Sometimes it's time to move on.

And, by the same token, sometimes it's time to return.

In 1977 I published *Burglars Can't Be Choosers,* the first of a series about one Bernie Rhodenbarr. Four more books followed in about as many years, and then after a few failed attempts at a sixth volume I stopped trying. I turned to other things, and the years passed, as they always seem to do.

Bernie was a hugely popular character, and whenever I made a personal appearance at a signing or conference, the first question I'd get (and often the fourth and twelfth as well) was when I would write another book about him. "Soon, I hope," I would say at first, but the years kept passing without another Burglar book, and I began saying that it was unlikely there'd be any more of them. "I'd like to write another," I would say, "but I don't think it will happen. Though I certainly don't rule it out."

And what about Tanner, someone would occasionally ask. Any chance of a new Tanner book?

"No," was always my reply. "No, there's a slim chance of a new Burglar book, but Tanner's done."

And, after eleven Rhodenbarrless years, I did in fact produce *The Burglar Who Traded Ted Williams,* and there have been four more since then. Bernie's reappearance led to still more readers wondering if Tanner as well might be in for a revival.

"No," I said. "Never happen."

Shows what I know.

Here's how it happened. A paperback publisher had arranged to reprint the Tanner books, and sent me galleys of the first two titles, to see if there was anything that needed to be changed. I was pretty sure I didn't want to change anything—you pull one thread and the whole sweater unravels—but I figured it wouldn't hurt me to read the books.

So I did, and what happened was I remembered just how much fun it had been to write them. Now memory's a curious thing. It's never as accurate as one thinks, for one thing, and for another one tends to remember the more pleasant aspects of an event and forget the bad part. (And a good thing, let me tell you, or nobody would ever have a second child or run a second marathon.) So the books probably weren't quite that much fun to write, but that's how I recalled them. And in fact there had been an insouciance about my writing all those years ago; if it was often lamentably careless, it was as well delightfully carefree. These were fun, I told myself all those years later. And I guess they were.

So why not sign up for some more fun? Why not write some more about Tanner?

Alas, I didn't see how I possibly could. For one thing, the fellow was a Korean war veteran. By now he was twenty-eight years older than he'd been in *Me Tanner, You Jane*, which would make him well up in his sixties, and a tad long in the tooth for all of that hopping in and out of various beds and across various borders. Some series characters stay the same age forever, and Bernie Rhodenbarr isn't a day older than he was in his first appearance, and no one has ever been bothered by this heroic defiance of Time's winged chariot. But Tanner, rooted in historical and geopolitical realities (or unrealities, as you prefer) struck me as the sort of character who had to exist in real time.

And, even if one was prepared for an action-adventure hero old enough to collect Social Security, how to explain his quarter-century absence? What the hell had he been doing since we saw him last? Sleeping? Not likely, since sleeping was the one thing he didn't do at all.

Nope, I decided. There was no way to write more Tanner books. The folks at Dutton would be delighted if I did, as it would certainly kick-start the reprint series, but that wasn't reason enough to do it. There were real impediments here, and no way around them. So I shrugged, as I often do, and said the hell with it, as I often do.

But I forgot to inform my subconscious mind.

What happened was I went to a concert. It was at Lincoln Center, and the New York Philharmonic was playing something or other, but all I recall of the evening is the idea that came to me. There are three things that happen to me at concerts, and I can't cause them to happen, nor can I stop them from happening. One is sleep, and another is being absorbed in the music, and the third is a state where I'm very much awake but done concentrating on the music, so that my mind wanders.

Sometimes, wandering, it produces (or allows the reception of) ideas.

Which is what happened that particular evening. All at once I thought of a way to account for the twenty-eight year gap since we'd last heard from Tanner, and to keep him the age he'd been when we saw him last. The world had moved on, while he'd remained unchanged, fixed—yea, verily, *frozen* in time.

Once I had the idea, a world of possibilities opened, all of them deliciously Tanneresque. I couldn't wait to write the book.

I decided to set it in Burma, a country Lynne and I had visited a couple of months earlier, at a time when I had not the slightest idea I'd even want to set a book there, let alone one starting Evan Tanner. And I decided to write it in Ireland, in the town of Listowel, in north Kerry.

If I did so today, I'd take along a laptop. But this was just long enough ago to make me nervous about trying to use a computer that far from home. So instead I took a pen and some legal pads and sat down at a table in my room at the Listowel Arms and wrote the book in longhand.

(The computer, incidentally, is blamed for the fact that books are longer than they used to be. Writing's become so much easier that writers are self-indulgent, and natter on at greater length than they ought to. Well, I may well be self-indulgent, and I very likely natter on longer than I ought to, but that trip to Ireland proved that the computer has precious little to do with it. I wrote every word with a ballpoint pen, and my hand ached at the end of each day's session, and still the bloody book ran 90,000 words, which made it almost half again as long as Tanner's earlier adventures, each of which had been pounded out far less effortfully on a Smith-Corona portable. So don't blame the computer, my friend. Blame the windy old fart who's tapping away at it.)

And will there be any additional Tanner novels? Is there a chance we'll hear from him again?

Well, I'll tell you, I've learned, as they say, never to say never. Tanner surprised the daylights out of me by reappearing after twenty-eight years. The fellow would appear to have the life-cycle of a cicada. So look for him sometime in 2026.

MORE ABOUT TANNER

The foregoing eight-part discourse is probably as much of an introduction as Evan Tanner requires, but there's more. Subterranean Press published first hardcover editions of *The Scoreless Thai* and *Tanner's Tiger*, and I wrote afterwords for both. And here they are:

THE SCORELESS THAI

In 1967, in the middle of January, I went to JFK and caught a plane headed for Dublin. I had a Prohibition-era sterling silver hip flask in my pocket, filled with John Jameson, and if that isn't a case of carrying coals to Newcastle, I don't know what is. It hardly mattered, as I had two short snorts from the thing, dozed off, woke up when the plane was touching down, and left the flask in the seat pocket. Some son of a bitch got a nice surprise.

I carried my attaché case off the plane and went through Immigration and Customs. The guy at Customs told me to collect my baggage first, but all I had was the attaché case. I opened it to reveal a pair of shoes, a pair of socks, a pair of undershorts, and a stack of typed pages. He asked how long I planned to stay.

"Indefinitely," I said.

The Irish are a hospitable race. He let me in, and I got a room at the Homestead, a bed and breakfast in Amiens Street, near Connolly Station. I settled in, and that day or the next I found an office-supplies firm nearby in Talbot Street where I rented an office-model typewriter. They sold me a ream of typing paper, too. The sheets were at once longer and narrower than the US standard, but so what? I put the typewriter on a table and drew up a chair and went to work.

I'd brought along the first 160 pages of the third Evan Tanner novel, which I would eventually call *The Lettish Tomatoes* only to see Fawcett issue it as *Tanner's Twelve Swingers*. I got up every morning, ate my eggs and sausages and drank my tea, then sat down at the typewriter, and a month later the book was done. I could say more about that month in Dublin, and about the writing of that book, and I probably will, one of these days, in another afterword. Suffice it to say that, one afternoon in Eaton's bookstore in O'Connell Street, I came upon a book called *Teach Yourself Latvian*, which, now that I think on it, sounds more like a curse than an invitation. "Go shit in your hat!" "Teach yourself Latvian!" "Arrggghhhh, you got me there, you bastard. . ."

I taught myself enough Latvian to salt the book with words

and phrases, undeterred by the fact that not one reader in ten thousand would know or care whether they were accurate or not. No matter. The book was done. I packed it up and took it to the Post Office—yes, *that* post office, the GPO on O'Connell Street, focal point of the Easter Rising of 1916. And I addressed it to my agent in New York and put stamps on it and mailed it off.

Now what?

It's not uncommon for me to go away to write something. I seem better able to concentrate on the work when I'm isolated with it. In recent years I've written at writers' colonies in Virginia and Illinois, in a hotel in San Francisco's Tenderloin, aboard a clipper ship and a Norwegian coastal steamer, and, a couple of years ago, in the Listowel Arms, in County Kerry.

But that's not why I went to Ireland that January of 1967. I didn't go there to write a book. I wrote the book while I was there, because writing is what I do, and I had to do something. But the reason I went there was to get the hell away from my life. I'd been married for almost seven years, and then I'd plunged into a remarkably messy and turbulent affair, and I'd moved out and moved back and moved out and moved back again, and I had reached a point where, as a less delicate soul might phrase it, I didn't know whether to shit or go blind. So I went to Ireland, and finished the book, and tried to figure out what to do next.

I decided to go see something of the country. I'd first come to Ireland in the fall of 1964, and had fallen in love with the place; ever since I'd had fantasies of moving there, and now had it in mind that I might never go back, that I'd scout out the best place to settle and then send for my wife. Or the other woman. Or something.

I bought a truly cumbersome knapsack and packed it with

the clothes I'd bought, and I took a bus as far as Bray, then hitchhiked down along the southeastern coast. It was slow going; there'd been an incident a few weeks earlier, a hitchhiker who pulled a knife on a motorist and made him go several miles out of his way. (This got a lot of play in the papers, and made an impression on the populace. There wasn't much crime in Ireland in those days, and it didn't take a lot to cause a stir.) Consequently, there was a period of a week or two when motorists were leery of hitchhikers, before the episode faded from the public consciousness.

So when I got to Wicklow Town I bought a bicycle.

I won't say it was the worst idea I ever had. The remarkably messy and turbulent affair, for instance, was far worse. But the bicycle surely ranked in the top ten or twelve. It had three gears, all of them identical, as far as I could tell. And riding it was an awkward proposition when one was encumbered by a cumbersome knapsack. Still, it might have been bearable, but for two things—the weather and the hills.

All it did was rain. There are people who will tell you that's all it ever does in Ireland, and by and large they're right. It was certainly all it did while I was on my bicycle. It rained while I was going uphill, and it rained while I was going downhill. I don't know that it rained when I was on level ground, because the situation never arose. I was always either going uphill—walking the bicycle, because it was impossible to pedal that bike up those hills—or I was going downhill, picking up speed, zooming along out of control, and knowing that, exhilarating as it all felt, I was very shortly going to be killed.

Though it certainly seemed longer, I was only on the bike three or four days. I went to Wexford Town, and then to Gorey.

I was on my way from Gorey to Enniscorthy when a truck pulled up alongside me. It was the couple at whose B&B I'd stayed in Gorey, and they offered me a lift. Afterward, it struck me that they hadn't been going anywhere; they'd gotten in the truck and gone for a ride so that they could save me from drowning. They felt sorry for me, and I can understand why.

In Enniscorthy I stayed with a Mrs. Twomey. I was there for three days, and sometime during the third day I figured out why. Enniscorthy was an interesting town, the site of a noteworthy battle of the 1798 Rising, and I did go to the museum and look at old farm implements, so it wasn't as if there was nothing to do there. But I hung around and hung around because I didn't want to get back on the damned bike.

Meanwhile my landlady's son was admiring the bike, and I was encouraging him. I let his mother know that I might be convinced to sell it to her. I'd paid twenty-five or thirty pounds for it—the pound was at $2.40 at the time—and I'd owned it for less than a week, and had walked it up the hills. If I could get, say, half of what I'd paid for it. . .

She decided she couldn't afford it, for all that it was a fair price. So I made her what Mario Puzo had not yet taught us to call an offer she couldn't refuse. I told her she could have it for what I owed for my three days' bed and breakfast, which would have been something like five or six quid.

She went for it, the silly woman. If she'd held out I'd have let the kid have it for free.

I stood at the roadside and held out my thumb, and now it was easy. A fellow gave me a ride right away and took me all the way to Mitchelstown, in County Cork, where he stopped to show off a brand-new pork processing plant where he had installed some machinery. He bought me lunch, and when he got to the Cork City turnoff he parked the car, got out of it with me, and flagged down another car and importuned the driver to run me in to Cork. "He's a good lad," he assured the fellow. "You'll have no trouble with him."

I was a few days in Cork City and took a bus to Bantry, in West Cork, on Bantry Bay. I stayed at a crappy bed and breakfast for a few days, and then they told me I had to leave, as there were laborers in town and they could put three or four lads in my room and collect three or four times as much for it. That didn't seem right to me, but I didn't like the place enough to argue. I moved down the street to the Anchor Hotel, run by a man who'd hitchhiked around the world. When he got as far as New Zealand he met an absolutely smashing girl, married her, and brought her back to West Cork to help him run the hotel.

It was a nice place, and I settled in. After a few days I found a store that sold typewriters. I bought an Olivetti Lettera and some typing paper and started work on a new Tanner book. I wrote what I recall as twenty or thirty pages, but, looking at the book now, I have no way of telling just how much of it was written in Ireland. The first chapter, certainly, and maybe the second chapter as well.

Then one day, about two months after I'd arrived in Dublin and one month after I'd finished the previous book, it was time to go home. I took the typewriter back to the store where I'd bought it and tried to sell it back to him. He agreed to take it on consignment, and to send me a check when he sold it. I'm still waiting, but who's to say I'll never see the money? Sure, he had an honest face. . .

I hitched rides to Shannon and flew home, and life went on.

My then-wife and I were living in New Brunswick, New Jersey, in a fine old house on Stratford Place, and every day I went upstairs to the attic room I used as an office, and after a month or two the book was done.

Since one of its chief characters was a Siamese lad who had no luck with the ladies, I called it *The Scoreless Thai*. Gold Medal published it as *Two For Tanner*, and I was flabbergasted. I couldn't even figure out what it was supposed to mean. Two for Tanner? What two? Which two? Huh?

Idiots.

Before the book came out, they sent me galleys. (They didn't always.) And I proofread them. (I didn't always.) And, in Chapter Four, I noted, among the CIA fronts pointed out to Tanner by Barclay Houghton Hewitt, was a tobbo shop.

A tobbo shop? What the hell was that?

I checked the manuscript, and I'd written tobacco, not tobbo. I started to change it, then stopped myself. The word, after all, had a nice ring to it. Any fool could point out a tobacco shop in Bangkok, but only someone with intimate knowledge of the city would know about the tobbo shops, right?

So I left it alone.

And, ever since, I've come across other works of fiction by other diligent researchers who've included the tobbo shops of Bangkok as local color.

What can I say? I finally did get to Thailand a couple of years ago, some thirty years behind Tanner, and there were tobbo shops all over the place. You had to look hard to spot them, but they were there.

* * *

TANNER'S TIGER

I think it's fair to say that the character and lifestyle of Evan Tanner represented a good measure of wishful thinking on the author's part.

Just compare the two. Tanner, whose sleep center was destroyed in Korea, is not merely conscious but energetically and productively awake twenty-four hours a day. He spends his time studying languages, for which he has a natural aptitude, and earns a living writing theses and term papers for lazy students. When an assignment or a whim moves him to action, he travels all over the world, slipping across borders effortlessly, talking to strangers and fellow conspirators in their own languages, and having adventures left and right. He even gets laid a lot.

The author, on the other hand, was a textbook example of None Of The Above. He needed his eight hours every night, and was positively sluglike in his inertia for much of his waking hours. For all that he had three years of Latin and two years of Spanish in high school, it was all he could do to make himself understood in his native tongue. He was ill-equipped to write theses or term papers for anyone else, having demonstrated an inability to do so for himself.

Nor was he given to hopscotching the globe. He'd been to Canada many times—he grew up in Buffalo, right there on the border, and his family would cross the Peace Bridge several times every summer to spent a day at the Canadian beaches. He'd been to Mexico once, with dire results; he and his friend, tear-gassed and swept up by the Federales when they blundered into a political demonstration on the way back to their Guadalajara hotel, were held in jail overnight, then left with just enough cash to get them back to the border.

Not long before writing the first Tanner book, *The Thief Who Couldn't Sleep*, he finally crossed the ocean, visiting Ireland, Scotland, and England. There at least he could understand what people were saying—except in Hawick, on the border of Scotland and Northumberland, where he spent two hours in a pub next to a talkative Geordie and could not decipher one sentence in twenty.

As for his romantic adventures, well, never mind.

I think it's about time for me to quit talking about myself in the third person. I'm not a professional athlete, after all. Suffice it to say that my life and Tanner's were vastly different, and I'd have traded with him in a hot second.

Some readers, especially those who have trouble with the whole concept of fiction, think a writer has to have vast quantities of real-world experience. How can you write about what you haven't seen and done?

Well, that's nonsense. Fiction is not autobiography, nor is it journalism. The fiction writer's single most valuable asset—aside, perhaps, from a working knowledge of the language in which he purports to tell his story—is his imagination. It is the source not only of the ideas for his stories but of virtually everything involved in their development. He works it all out in his imagination, and he gets it down on paper, and Bob's your uncle.

Still, there's something to be said for having a certain familiarity with the places where one's stories are set. In book after book, I had Tanner bouncing all over Eastern Europe, with occasional forays to Asia and Africa. I hadn't been to these places, and, again unlike Tanner, I wasn't that diligent in my research. I have an old-trunk-in-the-attic type of memory, and retain a lot of weird information that proves useful in chronicling Tanner's adventures, but my real research was limited at best. If it wasn't in the 1948 edition of the Encyclopedia Britannica, and if it didn't show up on a map in the Britannica Atlas, Tanner didn't know about it.

Fortunately, I was in the happy position of Edgar Rice Burroughs writing books set in Africa—or on Mars. I.e., damn few of my readers had been to Lithuania or Afghanistan or Thailand or Modonoland. If I got something wrong, well, who'd know? In a sense, my own appalling ignorance gave me enormous freedom. My Yugoslavia (and thus Tanner's) could be whatever I imagined it to be, whatever best suited my narrative purposes. I wasn't hamstrung by the facts.

Tanner's Tiger was the fifth book in the series. It was the middle volume of three Tanner books published in 1968, which suggests it was written in late 1967 or very early in 1968.

The idea for the book came while Expo '67 was running in Montreal. It struck me that it would be interesting if Tanner, who had been hopping blithely from country to country, often with false papers or no papers at all, should have difficulty crossing the easiest border of all, between the US and Canada. And wouldn't it be ironic if this should happen on a pure pleasure trip, with no political agenda involved? Suppose Minna cajoled him into taking her to Expo, and suppose he got turned back at the border, and suppose he had to sneak into Canada, and then—

Well, you get the idea. I mean, you've read the book, right? You're not one of those people who read the afterword first, are you?

I didn't know what would happen after that, but neither did I sit down and start writing. Instead I took an action that was a radical departure from my usual procedure.

I went to Canada.

To Montreal, to be specific, where I spent three or four days wandering around the city and the Expo fairgrounds, going from pavilion to pavilion.

The Cuban pavilion made quite an impression on me. It was, I can assure you, just as described in the novel, although (as far as I know) there was no trapdoor in the floor for the purpose of capturing black Americans.

Aside from the Cuban pavilion, I recall very little of my trip to Montreal. I remember sitting in a coffee shop, slightly drunk, in the company of a drunken Montrealer who ordered iced coffee with lemon. It was, he insisted, more refreshing that way. (I still order it like that myself once in a while, but never without an argument from the waitress. "It's refreshing," I say.) I remember making the acquaintance of a working girl from Newfoundland. (Tanner would have been proud of me.) And I remember trying to find an address the pronunciation of which I could not begin to guess. It was something like 874 Pie ix, and I didn't know whether the first work was English or French, and whether the ix was a Roman numeral or a word or an abbreviation. I went up to somebody on the street with the address written out on a scrap of paper and pretended to be a deaf mute, putting a finger across my lips, then pointing to the address, and eliciting elaborate gestures in response from the poor soul I'd stopped. (Marcel Marceau would not have been proud of me. Tanner would have been horrified.)

Then I went home and wrote the book.

About the title:

I don't remember what I called it. After having had two titles in a row changed, and not for the better, I may not have called it anything at all. I sent it to Henry Morrison, my then-agent, and he sent it to Knox Burger, my then-editor, and somewhere down the line I got a call from Henry. The book was fine, he reported, and they wanted to call it *Tanner's Tiger*.

"That sounds okay," I said, "except. . .wait a minute. What tiger?"

"Arlette," Henry said. "Remember the girl?"

"Vividly," I said. "But what does she have to do with a tiger?"

"Nothing," Henry said, "except for the fact that she's described as wearing a full-length tigerskin coat."

"Oh," I said. "This is weird, Henry, but I don't remember the coat at all."

"That's because you haven't written it yet," he said. "But you will. They want her to have the coat, so that they can call the book *Tanner's Tiger*, and then they can show her on the cover *wearing* the coat, and they think it'll be great."

"Oh," I said.

"You can do it, can't you?"

I could and did. It was, I must say, by no means the stupidest thing any publisher asked me to do, nor was it the stupidest change I agreed to. While I can't know that it added anything to the finished product, what could it hurt?

And, of course, you won't find the coat on the cover of the Gold Medal paperback. Instead she's wearing a skimpy two-piece tigerskin bathing suit.

Go figure. . .

Short Stories

Back in 1977 I wrote a short story about a criminous criminal attorney named Ehrengraf. Fred Dannay, who published the story in Ellery Queen's Mystery Magazine, liked Ehrengraf and encouraged me to write more. In 1994 Jim Seels brought out the existing Ehrengraf stories in a limited edition, with the title *Ehrengraf For the Defense.* Ed Hoch provided a very generous introduction for the volume, in which he recounted his own experiences in this regard with Fred. My afterword, which follows here, picked up on what Ed had to say. I should note that there have been a couple more stories in the series since Seels brought out his book; all of them (so far!) may be found in *Enough Rope.*

Amazing what you find out. To think that Fred Dannay was once interested in a continuation of Melville Davisson Post's Randolph Mason stories! To think that Ed Hoch once undertook to provide it!

I of course had no idea. When I wrote the first Ehrengraf story in 1977, I didn't know anything more about Melville Davisson Post than his name. Fred Dannay was crazy about the story, and heralded Ehrengraf as a lineal descendant of Randolph Mason.

I didn't know what the hell he was talking about. And I may have been just a tiny bit sensitive on the subject. Because, while I hadn't pilfered any ideas from Post, the first Ehrengraf story was an example of what I've elsewhere called Creative Plagiarism.

I hadn't stolen the character. Ehrengraf was my own creation, sprung from my high forehead like Athena from the brow of Jupiter. No, what I'd stolen was the plot itself.

And not from Melville Davisson Post, either. I'd lifted it from Fletcher Flora.

I don't remember the title of the story, or just where and when it appeared. I'd guess it was published in *Manhunt,* probably in the mid-to-late 1950s. While the details of the story have long since left my memory, I recall that it concerned a good friend of the narrator, who was in jail, charged with murdering a young woman. The narrator, operating on the principle that greater love hath no man than to lay down someone else's life for a friend, gets his buddy off the hook by committing another murder or two with the identical MO. The friend, securely in jail at the time, has an unshakable alibi, and is thus off the hook for the first murder, which he did in fact commit.

I read the story, I liked the story, I forgot about the story, and years later I remembered it again and thought what a pleasure it would be to write that story. There was only one problem. Someone had already written it.

So I thought some more about it, and started poking it and probing it, looking for ways to change it. I decided that an artful attorney would make a good hero, and it struck me that he'd be particularly well motivated if he worked, as negligence lawyers do, upon a contingency basis. Martin Ehrengraf took shape at once, the minute I started writing the first paragraph. All his traits and mannerisms were somehow there from the beginning, as if he'd been waiting patiently for me to sit down and write about him.

I didn't intend him as a series character, but characters have frequently surprised me in this fashion over the years, and I don't think a month passed after I'd written the first Ehrengraf story before I found myself writing a second.

Fred Dannay was the first editor to see the first Ehrengraf story, and he snapped it up for EQMM. *He* wasn't surprised when there was a second story, and did indeed hail my little lawyer as the reincarnation of Randolph Mason, and went on buying the stories as they rolled out of my typewriter. He passed on one, "The Enrengraf Obligation," finding it too gory for his taste. Rather than rewrite it for him, I sent it off to *Mike Shayne* magazine, where I sold it for the price of a dinner, and not a great dinner, either. Fred bought the next one, and the one after that, and after his death in 1982 Eleanor Sullivan continued to take what Ehrengraf stories I managed to write.

But there haven't been all that many of them. Early on, Otto Penzler told me he'd like to publish a collection of the Ehrengraf stories as soon as I got enough of them written to fill a book. That sounded good to me.

It never happened.

Ehrengraf's problem, you see, is that he has a severely limited range. There haven't been that many story ideas that have worked for him. I haven't wanted to write the same story over and over, and have waited for variations to suggest themselves. There have thus far been only these eight which appear together now for the first time.

I can't tell you there'll never be another. I write these lines in May of 1994, the publication month of *The Burglar Who Traded Ted Williams*, Bernie Rhodenbarr's first book-length adventure in over a decade. If Bernie could come back after so long an absence, I can hardly rule out an eventual future appearance of the wily Martin Herod (or Harrod) Ehrengraf. I wouldn't hold my breath, but I'm not going to say it'll never happen.

For now, though—and perhaps forever—all the Ehrengraf stories are available in a single volume, arranged in the order in which they were written. I hope you like the dapper little fellow. I can tell you I had a good time writing about him.

ENOUGH ROPE

Just the other day a Facebook friend informed me that he'd received a Kindle for Christmas. "And the first thing I'll buy for it," he said, "is *Enough Rope*, because this way I'll actually be able to read it without wrecking my wrists."

It is, no question, a huge doorstop of a book. At the time I thought of it as my complete short stories, but it wasn't, and it's even less so now. Since then Crippen & Landru brought out two limited-edition collections of earlier work, *One Night Stands* and *The Lost Cases of Ed London*, and HarperCollins subsequently combined the two books as *One Night Stands and Lost Weekends*. And I've written more stories which will eventually have a book of their own. But here's what I had to say about *Enough Rope:*

"Eighty-three stories?" My friend gave me a look. "That's not a book," he said. "That's a skyscraper."

It's a handful, too, as you've no doubt already noticed yourself, and I'm conscious as I prepare these introductory remarks that I'm only making the damned thing longer with every word I write. This book was very nearly entitled *Long Story Short,* and it's been observed that, when you hear the words "to make a long story short," it's already too late.

But I digress, and not for the first time. A short story collection seems to cry out for an introduction, especially when it's a huge doorstop of a thing like this one, and especially when it represents one person's entire output of short fiction over a career that began in (gulp!) 1957.

Well, virtually complete. . .

My earliest stories, collected a few years ago in a signed limited edition (*One Night Stands,* Crippen & Landru), have been purposely omitted. I don't think much of them—which puts me in the majority, I'd have to say—and, while I'm not unwilling for collectors and specialists to have them, they don't belong in this book. (I've made one exception, my first published story, called "You Can't Lose". It seemed worth including, if only as a curiosity.)

Two more recent shorter fictions, "Speaking of Lust" and "Speaking of Greed", have also been omitted. Each is the title novella in a volume of the Seven Deadly Sins anthology series, and, when all seven novellas have been written and published, they'll be gathered into a single volume. I'm very fond of the two written to date—but they're long, running around 20,000 words each, and they don't belong here.

And, come to think of it, my episodic novel *Hit Man* is essentially a collection of ten short stories, and that constituted a quandary all its own. If I were to include them all, I'd be folding a full book into this one, and making people buy it a second time. If I left them all out, well, I'd be passing up the chance to include one story that was shortlisted for the Edgar Allan Poe award and two others that won it outright. Some authors might be modest enough to omit such stories, and even to leave off mentioning the awards, but I am not of their number.

So I've compromised, and included those three of the ten, along with two more Keller stories—"Keller's Horoscope", extracted from the second Keller novel, *Hit List,* for publication in a German anthology, and "Keller's Designated Hitter", written for an anthology of baseball stories and otherwise unpublished. If there's a third book about Keller, perhaps it will be included. Then again, perhaps not. At any rate, it's here.

Once I'd selected the stories, I had to put them in order.

As far as I can see, there are three accepted ways to organize collections of short fiction. You can line them up in the order they were written, you can alphabetize them by title, or you can place them here and there like paintings in a gallery, trying to arrange them so that they'll complement one another.

The last is altogether beyond me—how the hell do I

know in what order you'll enjoy coming upon these stories? And chronological order is out of the question, because I couldn't possibly recall precisely when each story was written. Alphabetical order has always made perfect sense to me, it's so deliciously arbitrary and yet so marvelously unequivocal. How better to construct a sheer hodgepodge with the illusion of order?

But there's another variable to weigh in the balance, and that's that some of my stories are about series characters, and they really ought to be set off by themselves. And I do recall the order in which the series stories were written, and they really ought to be arranged in that order.

So here's the plan:

The stories which appeared in my three previously published collections, *Sometimes They Bite*, *Like a Lamb to Slaughter*, and *Some Days You Get the Bear*, appear first, in one great alphabetically ordered jumble.

The groups of stories which follow—about Martin Ehrengraf, Chip Harrison, Keller, Bernie Rhodenbarr, and Matthew Scudder—appear chronologically. Many of these showed up in the three above-named collections, but quite a few did not, and these are collected here for the first time: "The Ehrengraf Presumption," "The Ehrengraf Riposte," "The Ehrengraf Affirmation," and "The Ehrengraf Reverse;" "As Dark as Christmas Gets;" "Keller's Horoscope" and "Keller's Designated Hitter;" "The Burglar who Smelled Smoke;" and "The Night and the Music," "Looking for David," "Let's Get Lost," and "A Moment of Wrong Thinking".

Next are eleven new non-series stories. And, last and least, is an old story, indeed a first story, *You Can't Lose*, sold to *Manhunt* in the summer of 1957 and published in February, 1958.

* * *

And is that it?

Well, I hope not. I still get an enormous amount of satisfaction out of writing short stories, and I still find things I haven't done and try to work out ways to do them.

There is one thing I've noticed over the years, and maybe it's worth comment. It is, simply, that the stories have grown longer over time. In the early days I had to work at it to stretch a story to 3,000 words—and that was when I had every incentive to write long, as every word I used meant another cent and a half in my pocket. Now, when I tend to get paid by the story rather than by the word, I have to work even harder to hold them to two to three times that length.

(The same's true for books, and you hear people blame computers for making it easier to go on and on. I thought that might be it, until I wrote *Tanner on Ice*, the first Tanner novel in twenty-eight years, and found it running half again as long as its predecessors. I couldn't blame a computer, either, as I wrote the thing with a ballpoint pen on a stack of legal pads.)

Not long ago I read a thoughtful and perceptive introduction to a collection called *Here's O'Hara*, by Albert Erskine, John O'Hara's longtime editor. He noted that the more recent stories were substantially longer than the earlier ones, and said that they were also better. He wouldn't be foolish enough to argue that they were better because they were longer, Erskine wrote, but thought it was fair to contend that they were longer because they were better.

I know that's true for O'Hara, and I'd like to think it's true of my work as well. And maybe it is, maybe I write longer these days because my characters and situations are more richly conceived, and I consequently have more to say about them.

Or perhaps I'm just turning into a wordy old bastard. Tell you what—you decide.

ONE NIGHT STANDS AND LOST WEEKENDS

Here's what I had to say about the early stories collected in Crippen & Landru's edition of *One Night Stands*:

In 1956, from the beginning of August through the end of October, I lived in Greenwich Village and worked in the mail room at Pines Publications. I was a student at Antioch College, in Yellow Springs, Ohio, which sounds like a hell of a commute, but that's not how it worked. At Antioch students spent two terms a year studying on campus and two terms working at jobs the school arranged for them, presumably designed to give them hands-on experience in their intended vocational area. Like a majority of students, I had spent my entire freshman year on campus. Now, at the onset of my second year, I was ready to begin my first co-op job. I knew I wanted to be a writer, so I went through the school's list and picked a job at a publishing house.

Pines published a paperback line, Popular Library, a batch of comic books, and a couple dozen magazines, including some of the last remaining pulps in existence. (*Ranch Romances*, I recall, was one of them. It was what the title would lead you to believe.) I worked five days a week from nine to five, shunting interoffice mail from one desk to another, and doing whatever else they told me to do. My weekly salary was forty bucks, and every Friday I got a pay envelope with $34 in it.

I lived in the Village, at 54 Barrow Street, where I shared a one-bedroom apartment with two other Antioch co-ops. My share of the monthly rent was $30, so I guess it fit the traditional guideline of a week's pay. I know I never had any money, but I never missed any meals, either, and God knows it was an exciting place to be and an exciting time to be there. (I was eighteen, and on my own, so I suppose any place would have been exciting, but at the time I thought the Village was the best place in the world. Now, all these years later, I haven't changed my mind about that.)

I didn't do much writing during those months. I'd realized three years earlier that writing was what I wanted to do, and every now and then I actually wrote something. Poems, mostly, and story fragments. I sent things to magazines and they sent them back. At Antioch, I taped the rejection slips on the wall over my desk, like the heads of animals I'd slain. Sort of.

One weekend afternoon, I sat down at the kitchen table on Barrow Street and wrote "You Can't Lose." It was pretty much the way it appears here, but it didn't end. It just sort of trailed off. I showed it to a couple of friends. I probably showed it to a girlfriend, in the hope that it would get me laid, and it probably didn't work. Then I forgot about it, and the end of October I went back to campus.

Where at some point I remembered the story and dug it out and sent it to a magazine called *Manhunt*. All I knew about *Manhunt* was that most of the stories in Evan Hunter's collection *The Jungle Kids* had first appeared in its pages. I'd admired those stories, and it struck me that a magazine that would publish them might like my story. So I sent it off, and it stayed there for a while, and then back it came.

With a note enclosed from the editor. He liked it, but pointed out that it didn't have an ending, and that it rather needed one. If I could come up with a twist ending, a snapper ending, he'd like to see it again. So I found a newsstand that carried

Manhunt, bought a copy, read it, and wrote a new ending, one which at least proved I'd read O. Henry's "The Man at the Top." (My narrator ends with the triumphant boast that his ill-gotten gains are due to increase dramatically, because he's just invested the whole thing in some goldmine stock. Or something.)

I sent this off, and it came back with another note, saying the new ending was predictable and didn't really work, but thanks for trying. And that was that.

Then several months later the school year was coming to a close, and I was due to head off to Cape Cod and find a co-op job on my own. One night near the end of term I couldn't sleep, and I lay there thinking, and thought of the right way to finish the story. I went home to Buffalo to visit my folks, drove out to Cape Cod, and wrote a new ending for the story. The acceptance process was slow—*Manhunt* had what we've since learned to call a cash-flow problem—but, long story short, they bought it. Paid a hundred bucks for it.

My first sale.

I left the Cape after a month or so and wound up back in New York, where I got a job as an editor at a literary agency, reading scripts and writing letters to wannabe writers, telling them how talented they were and how this particular story didn't work, but by all means send us another story and another reading fee.

I lived in a residential hotel on West 103rd Street, where my $65-a-month rent was again a fourth of my salary. And, nights and weekends, I wrote stories, which the agency I worked for submitted to various magazines. Most of the stories were crime fiction. I hadn't yet decided I was going to be a crime fiction writer—I don't know that that's a decision I ever made—but in the meantime I read extensively in the field. There was a shop on Eighth Avenue off Times Square where they sold back copies of *Manhunt* and other digest-sized magazines (*Trapped, Guilty, Off-Beat, Keyhole, Murder,* and so on) at two for a quarter. I bought every one of these I could find, and I read them cover to cover. Some I liked and some I didn't, but somewhere along the way I must have internalized the sense of what made a story, and I wrote some of my own.

They sold, most of them, sooner or later. Sometimes to *Manhunt,* but more often to its imitators. *Trapped* and *Guilty* paid a cent and a half per word, so they were the first choice after *Manhunt* passed. Then came Pontiac Publications, at a penny a word. (Their magazines had titles like *Sure Fire* and *Twisted* and *Off-Beat,* and every story title had an exclamation mark at the end. I longed to call a story "One Dull Night" so that they could call it "One Dull Night!")

After I'd been a month or so at the literary agency, it was clear to me I was learning more than I'd ever learn in college, and that I'd be crazy to stop now. So I dropped out and stayed right where I was. In the spring, I decided I'd learned as much as I was going to at the job, and that a student draft deferment was, after all, better than a poke in the eye with a sharp bayonet. I went back to Antioch.

By the time I got there, I was writing books. "Sex novels" was what we called them, though they'd now get labeled "soft-core porn." I wrote one to order the summer before I returned to Antioch, and the publisher wanted more. So that's what I did instead of classwork. And I also went on writing crime stories. At the end of that academic year, in the summer of 1959, I dropped out again, and this time it took. I started writing a book a month for one sex novel publisher, and other books for other publishers, and from that point the crime short stories were few and far between.

When Doug Green and I discussed bringing out a collection of these early stories, he brought up the subject of an introduction. "You can read through the stories," he said, "and write some sort of preface."

"One or the other," I said. "You decide which."

I have a lot of trouble looking at my early work. I rarely like the way it's written, and I especially dislike the glimpse it gives me of the unutterably callow youth who produced it. I like that kid and wish him well, but read what he wrote? The hell with that.

You know what? I'm *afraid* to read them. I'm scared I'll decide not to publish them after all, and it's too late for that.

So an uncharacteristic attack of honesty compels me to advise you that I am in the curious position of introducing you to a couple of dozen short stories which I myself haven't read in forty years.

Someone else suggested that some of the stories might require revision, because attitudes expressed in them are out-of-date and politically incorrect. No way, I told him. First of all, one of the few interesting things about them is that they're of their time. I'd much rather burn them than update them. And screw political rectitude, anyway. You want to go through *Huckleberry Finn* and change the name of Huck's companion to African-American Jim? Be my fucking guest, but leave me out of it.

A couple of things you might want to know:

1. A few of these stories, as indicated in the bibliographical notes at the back, were published under pen names. This only happened when I wound up with more than one story in the

same issue of a magazine. W. W. Scott, who edited *Trapped* and *Guilty*, would make up a pen name when this occurred, generally by working a variation on the author's usual byline. Thus "B. L. Lawrence." The guy at Pontiac asked what pen name to use in similar circumstances, and I provided the name "Sheldon Lord." Were there other pen names? Maybe, because there have been editors in the business who had house names which they used at such times. Maybe they used them on stories of mine. I don't think this ever happened, but at this point I'd have know way of knowing. And no reason whatever to care. . .

2. There's a story in here called "Look Death in the Eye" that deserves comment. It may strike some readers as curiously familiar. I wrote it way back when, while I was working for the literary agent, and it sold to Pontiac, and I lost all track of it. Didn't have a copy, didn't know where to find one.

And I found myself thinking about the story. What I really liked about it was the last line, and that, really, was all I remembered. So I recreated the story from memory, right up to the last line, which I recalled word for imperishable word. I hammered it out and sent it off to a fellow named Bruce Fitzgerald, who was editing a magazine called *For Women Only*. (It was a beefcake magazine, as it happens, composed of outtake photos from *Blueboy*, a gay magazine. The stories and articles interspersed among the nude male pix in *For Women Only* were ostensibly slanted to female readers, of which I doubt the magazine had more than twenty nationwide. The idea was that, by being purportedly for women, it could get on newsstands closed to gay publications, where its true audience would, uh, sniff it out. Its name notwithstanding, it was really for *men* only. Publishing is a wonderful business.)

Bruce liked the story, but felt it was a little too graphic for his female readers, even though we all knew they didn't exist. Could he use it without the last line?

Without the last line, of course, there's no story. And the only reason I wrote the story a second time was so that I could re-use the last line. So I displayed artistic integrity I never knew I had and withdrew the story. I don't know what difference I thought it would make, since nobody read anything in that magazine anyway, but for once I just couldn't stop myself from doing the right thing. *Gallery* wound up taking it, last line and all. It was published as "Hot Eyes, Cold Eyes," and was later included in my second collection, *Like a Lamb to Slaughter.*

3. The title deserves explanation. Most of these stories were written in a single sitting. I would get an idea and sit down at the typewriter and hammer it out. You can hold a short-story idea entirely in the mind, especially the sort of brief and uncomplicated story that most of these are. A weekday evening or a weekend afternoon was generally time enough to see one of these stories through to the end.

It still often is. I still write stories rapidly, and sometimes complete one in a single setting. The major difference, it seems to me, is that the gestation period has gotten a lot longer. I'll nowadays let a story idea percolate or ferment or stew for days or weeks or months. Back then I tended to strike as soon as the iron was hot, or, occasionally, before it had really warmed up.

I've had three collections of short stories published, plus a small-press collection of the Ehrengraf stories and *Hit Man*, an episodic novel comprising the Keller stories. *One Night Stands* consists of stories deliberately omitted from these collections (or ones I'd lost track of, but if I'd had them handy I'd still have left them out).

What have we got here, then? A box labeled "pieces of string too small to save"? If they weren't worth collecting, why have I collected them?

I've been guided by the same principle (or, some might argue, the same lack thereof) that has led me to republish some early crime novels that I'd be hard put to read without cringing. The fact that I can't read them with pleasure doesn't mean someone else couldn't, or shouldn't. I've decided it's not my job to judge my early work. Let other people make what they will of it.

Then too, I'm not unmindful of the interests of collectors and readers with a special interest in an author—in this instance, myself. I don't collect books, but I have other collecting interests, and I understand the mind set. Of course a collector would want a writer's early work, to read or simply to have and to hold, and why should I deprive him of the opportunity? And why shouldn't some scholar with a thesis to write have access to that early work?

At the same time, I don't think these stories are much good, or representative of my mature work. For God's sake, when I wrote these my typewriter still had training wheels on it. So I've decided *One Night Stands* should have limited distribution, going not to general readers but to collectors and specialists. Thus it's being published only in a limited collector edition, and not, as is generally the case with Crippen & Landru publications, in trade paperback as well.

Enough! This introduction has passed the 2,500-word mark, which makes it longer than many of the stories it's introducing. It's taken most of the morning to write it, too. May you, Dear

Reader, like the tomcat who had the affair with the skunk, enjoy these stories as much as you can stand.

And here's the introduction to Crippen & Landru's collection, *The Lost Cases of Ed London*:

He should probably stay lost.

In fact, you can argue that he never should have existed in the first place. I didn't set out to write about him. His first appearance was in a book originally called (albeit not by me) *Death Pulls a Doublecross,* and I was writing about another fellow named Roy Markham.

That wasn't my idea, either. The idea originated with someone at a paperback house called Belmont Books, where they'd arranged with some TV people to do a novel that would tie in with *Markham,* an episodic television series about a private eye with that name, played by Ray Milland.

TV tie-ins were standard paperback fare at the time. God knows why. The notion, I suppose, was that people who already knew the character from television would want to read more about him. The books were what you'd expect—uninspired and uninspiring.

At this point I'd written and sold one crime novel, *Mona,* slated for publication by Fawcett Gold Medal. I got the assignment to write about Roy Markham, and I wrote the book, and by the time I was done I found myself thinking that it was too good to waste on a Belmont TV tie-in for a $1,000 advance. I showed it to Henry Morrison, who was representing me at the time, and he agreed; he showed it to Knox Burger at Gold Medal, who had recently bought *Mona*, and he agreed, too.

I met Knox in his office on West Forty-fourth Street next to the Algonquin, and we talked about what it would take to change Roy Markham into somebody else. I recall that he took exception to the name Roy, maintaining that it brought to mind a lot of crackers who gave him a hard time in the service.

I went home and turned Roy Markham into Ed London, and made a couple of other changes that Knox suggested, and that I no longer recall. (This was in 1960. There is much of 1960 that I do not recall, and it's probably just as well.) The book went in, and the book came out, and that was that.

Except that I owed Belmont a TV tie-in, which I then had to write. I knocked it out, and they published it as *Markham*, and subtitled it *The Case of the Pornographic Photos*. (It has since been republished as *You Could Call It Murder*, even as *Death Pulls a Doublecross* has since been republished as *Coward's Kiss*. These are better titles, but I don't know that they're enough to transform this pair of sow's ears into silk purses, or even plastic ones.) Poor Belmont. The network pulled the plug on Ray Milland well before the book came out, so they had nothing to tie in with.

Meanwhile, I had a private eye. Ed London, private eye.

Lucky me.

Thing is, I'd been figuring all along that what I needed was a series character. I liked reading about the same character over and over, and figured I'd like writing about one, too. So, having published one book about

Ed London, I thought the thing to do was write more of them.

Turned out I couldn't. Blame it on my youth, or on my low estimate of self, but in those years I only managed to hit a mark if I was deliberately aiming below it. *Mona* started out as a pseudonymous sex novel for one of my regular crap publishers; a few chapters in I thought it might have potential, and changed its direction. Ed London's first appearance started out as a TV tie-in. But when I aimed high in the first place, I froze. There were a couple of abortive first chapters for a second Ed London novel, but that's as far as it got.

Except for these three novelettes.

I have precious little recollection of the circumstances of writing them. I believe they were all produced while I was living in a suburb of Buffalo in 1962–3, but who knows? I think, too, that they were all initially published in *Man's Magazine*, and at least some of them were reprinted a couple of years later by the same publisher in *Guy Magazine*.

When it came time to assemble the stories for *One Night Stands*, the three Ed London stories were nowhere to be found. I knew I'd written at least one and it seemed to me I'd written two, but I didn't have copies, and none had turned up, so that was that.

Then, after *One Night Stands* came out, the other stories began to turn up, thanks especially to Terry Zobeck and Lynn Munroe. It turned out there were three of them. Three! How did that happen?

And here they are. I can't delude myself for a moment with the notion that the literature of crime fiction is richer for their reappearance. I, however, will be a few dollars richer, and, crass bastard that I am, that strikes me as reason enough for bringing them out in this extremely attractive format. (It's a handsome volume, isn't it? Satisfying to pick up and hold in the hand, a pleasure to see on the bookshelf. Hey, nobody says you've got to *read* the damn thing.)

Enjoy!

Jill Emerson Novels

ENOUGH OF SORROW
AND
WARM AND WILLING

In 1963 I was living in Tonawanda, New York, a suburb of Buffalo, where I grew up. My then-wife and I moved there from New York City in early 1962, when our daughter Amy was practicing blowing out candles in anticipation of her first birthday. We'd been there a little more than a year when a second daughter, Jill, was born. (There would be a third daughter, Alison, but she doesn't come into the picture until 1969. I'm mentioning her here and now because I don't want her to feel neglected.)

At the time I was writing a pseudonymous book each month for Nightstand Books, and I wrote an extra book the month Jill was born so that I'd be able to pay the hospital and the obstetrician. And some months before she said her first word (it was either *translucent* or *phlegmatic*; her mother and I remember it differently) I had a disagreement with my agent that led to the abrupt termination of our relationship. As Nightstand was a closed shop, its entire list furnished by the Scott Meredith Literary Agency, I was going to have to figure out a way to make a living.

So I became a lesbian.

Now I suppose it's possible to argue that I'd been one all along. My first novel, written in the spring of 1958, was published by Fawcett Publication's Crest Books imprint; it concerned a young woman who'd come from her college graduation to Greenwich Village to have a sexual identity crisis. (I called it *Shadows,* and put my own name on it; Crest called it *Strange Are the Ways of Love,* and picked Lesley Evans as a pen name for me. Someone at Crest chose "Leslie" for its sexual ambiguity, and someone else changed the spelling to resolve the ambiguity. It was my first book, and I didn't know that you didn't have to let publishers push you around like that.)

I'd written that particular book because I figured I could. Over the preceding year or two I'd read perhaps a dozen lesbian novels, along with a pair of popular nonfiction works by Ann Aldrich, who turned out to be one of a great many pen names for Marijane Meaker. I'd been writing and selling short stories, mostly to the crime fiction magazines, but I wanted to write a novel. One morning I woke up with a hangover and the germ of an idea, and by the end of the day I had a chapter-by-chapter outline. A few weeks later I sat down and wrote the book. It took no more than two weeks; I was right to see very clearly that it was something I could do. My agent sent it to Crest, the premier publisher of that sort of book, and they took it. So there.

Now as to why this was a book I was able to write, well, you can puzzle that out if you want to, but don't look to me for an answer. But when my Nightstand connection cut out, and I had a wife and two kids to support, I decided to resume my career as a lesbian. I also decided, for reasons that elude me, to do so on the sly.

First, though, I had to write a book, and shortly I wrapped up *Warm and Willing*—although I didn't call it that. I forget what I did call it, but I remember that I hung some sort of title on it and wrapped it up and sent it off to John J. Plunkett, editor-in-chief at Midwood Tower. I enclosed a covering note from Jill Emerson, the pen name I'd chosen. I was renting an office at the time, about a quarter of a mile from my house in Tonawanda, and I used the office address.

I already knew Jill could get mail there. Before I wrote the book, I'd had Jill Emerson join an organization called the Daughters of Bilitis, the nation's first lesbian rights organization. I don't remember much about the outfit—Jill was never all that active a member—but they had a publication called *The Ladder*, and it came to my office, addressed to Jill, in a plain brown wrapper.

Now why did I submit this book over the transom? I'd written no end of books for Midwood, and they were not a closed market in the manner of Nightstand. All I had to do was get in touch with Plunkett, or his boss, publisher Harry Shorten, and say I was looking for work. Unsolicited over-the-transom submissions never get published, and they rarely even get read, so what made me think I had a chance?

Well, see, I was pretty good at this. And, in fact Jill got a letter of acceptance and the offer of a contract almost by return mail. Within a week or two, anyway. Before too long she'd written a portion and outline of a second novel, which Plunkett accepted, and which was published in due course by Midwood, this time with the title I'd slapped on it, *Enough of Sorrow*.

The title's from "Borrower," a 1918 poem by Mary Carolyn

Davies, a fine poet who's pretty much forgotten these days. Here's the full text:

> I sing of sorrow,
> I sing of weeping.
> I have no sorrow.
>
> I only borrow
> From some tomorrow
> Where it lies sleeping,
> Enough of sorrow
> To sing of weeping.

Those two books, *Warm and Willing* and *Enough of Sorrow*, are all Jill was destined to write for Midwood. A few years later she was back in business, writing three novels for Berkley's new line of erotic paperbacks. Then she wrote a big mainstream Bucks County novel, *The Trouble with Eden,* published by G. P. Putnam's Sons; I've always thought of it as the sort of thing John O'Hara might have done if he'd had no shame. And in 1975 Jill rounded things off with *A Week as Andrea Benstock,* a more ambitious mainstream novel set in my own home town of Buffalo, published by Arbor House, and serialized in *Redbook.*

If you read *Warm & Willing* first, I'm delighted you thought enough of it to have a look at Jill's second effort. I think *Enough of Sorrow* may dig a little deeper, and I hope you've enjoyed it.

A MADWOMAN'S DIARY

Jill Emerson began her career with a pair of sensitive lesbian novels in the mid-sixties and next wrote three determinedly erotic paperback originals for Berkley Books. If the books had one thing in common, besides their eager embrace of American literature's new sexual freedom, it was to be found in their structure. I had come to find the traditional novel limiting in its artificiality; I was drawn to books that that moved beyond the standard first- or third-person narrative.

Jill's first work for Berkley, *Three*, took the form of a diary. Her second, *Threesome*, was structurally the most ambitious of all; its three narrators, who comprise a sexual ménage à trois, have decided to collaborate on a novelization of their own experience, and the book we are reading is the one they are writing.

For a third book, I chose a return to the diary. The keeper of this diary is a young woman, discontented and more than a tad neurotic. I don't know that it's fair to call her mad, in either sense of the word, but I hung the title *A Madwoman's Diary* on it all the same. I'm sure I was echoing the title of Sue Kaufman's excellent novel *Diary of a Mad Housewife*, which I'd read and been hugely impressed by a couple of years earlier. I don't know that Ms. Kaufman's heroine could truly be described as mad either, but the title had worked well for her, and I reworded it and took it for my own.

If I took the title from one author, I stole the plot and character from another. I obtained my protagonist, my titular madwoman, not from another novel but rather from a work of nonfiction, specifically a collection of psychosexual case histories. Her background, her emotional makeup, her sexual acting out, indeed all the elements of the life she led, moved seamlessly from this case history into my novel.

Plagiarism? Well, I can see how you might think so, but I could argue otherwise. Because how can one steal what one already owns?

See, the collection of case histories was my work. It was I who had written up all the case histories in the volume, had in fact made them up out of whole cloth. The fabrication of human lives is after all part of the job description of a writer of fiction. That's what we do, and that's what I was doing when I wrote the various works of John Warren Wells.

First, years before there was John Warren Wells, there was Dr. Morton A. Benjamin of Chicago, Illinois. You may not have heard of him, and indeed it would be remarkable if you had, because the only people on earth who knew of his existence were an editor at Monarch Books and, later, an editor at Lancer Books. The public knew Mort Benjamin as Benjamin Morse, M.D., which is the name he put on the books he wrote—or would have written, if he'd ever existed in the first place.

I was the one who wrote the books. I made up his name and I made up his pen name and I made up all the characters in all the books he wrote. The books consisted of the stories of the doctor's patients and told how each person had gotten the way they were and how Dr. Morse led them out of the darkness and into, oh, hell, I don't know where he led them. Where do you go when you emerge from the darkness? Into the din and the glare, I suppose.

We never learned much about Benjamin Morse, not even his false real name, but it was evident that he was a kind and thoughtful therapist, and insightful and perceptive in the bargain. Now I had never been to a therapist at the time, and the only psychiatrist I knew was a man in Buffalo, New York. His two boys were in my scout troop, and he and his wife played bridge occasionally with my parents.

After one such evening at the doctor's home, my father reported that he thought the fellow was nuts. "The kids went upstairs around nine thirty," he said, "and fifteen minutes later they called down that they couldn't sleep. 'The boys can't sleep,' he announced. 'I'd better go give them each a sleeping pill.' And he did."

Ben Morse would never do a thing like that. Or Mort Benjamin, either. No fucking way.

I was all of twenty-two when I began life as Mort Benjamin, or Ben Morse, or whoever the hell I was. My then-agent, Henry Morrison, came to me with an assignment from Charles Heckelmann, the genius who would later come up with the notion of *Fidel Castro Assassinated* (now *Killing Castro*). Heckelmann wanted a doctor to write a book of case histories on female homosexuality, probably figuring this was a way to get on newsstands where lesbian novels wouldn't be tolerated.

Well, I'd already written lesbian fiction, so why not write some more in the sheep's clothing of nonfiction? Henry assured me it was legal to be a fake doctor, as long as I didn't usurp medical privileges by diagnosing or prescribing. So Ben Morse wrote *The Lesbian*, and a companion volume called *The Homosexual*, and, God help us, a marriage manual.

Then Heckelmann read a book called *The Power of Sexual Surrender,* by a psychiatrist named Marie Robinson—a real one, evidently. He decided Monarch ought to publish it—but since someone else already had, he wanted Dr. Morse to rip it off. Henry sold him on the notion of another doctor, one Walter C. Brown, as being better suited to the subject matter. Then he told me to get busy being Walter C. Brown.

I used a different typewriter. I wrote the book—God knows how, I couldn't really make out what Marie Robinson was getting at. And Heckelmann took it, but he told Henry he wasn't nuts about Walt Brown, that he just wasn't on the same level as Mort Benjamin. I could only conclude that he liked me better with a larger typeface, and that was the end of the short and happy life of Walter C. Brown.

John Warren Wells came into being after I split with the Scott Meredith Literary Agency. Benjamin Morse hadn't limited himself to Monarch and had done a book or two for Lancer, and I got in touch with Larry Shaw at Lancer, whom I knew through mutual friends in the Village. I said I was Dr. Benjamin's collaborator. I proposed a book—*Eros & Capricorn, a Cross-Cultural Survey of Sexual Techniques*. I wasn't sure what that meant, but it sounded good to Larry, who suggested that I might want to leave the good doctor out of this and do it on my own. Well, okay—and the name I came up with was John Warren Wells.

J. W. W. went on to produce a considerable body of work, most of it for Lancer but some for such A-list houses as NAL and Dell Publishing. For the better part of a year he had a monthly column in *Swank*, a magazine published by Lancer; it was something like *Penthouse Forum*, with letters from readers. I could tell you a great deal more about John Warren Wells, and may if I decide to epublish some of his work, but that's enough for now.

In one of the books for Lancer—and don't ask me which one, because I haven't the faintest idea—one of the fabricated case histories stayed with me. It came to mind when it was time for Jill Emerson to work up a third novel for Berkley. So I took this figment of my imagination, which I'd spun out as a supposedly true case history, and recycled it as a work of fiction, itself presented in the form of a document—a diary.

The book went pretty well. It evolved, of course, and owed less to the Wells case history by the time it was done, but it seemed right to acknowledge the debt, if obliquely. Jill did the right thing, and the book bears this dedication:

To JOHN WARREN WELLS
a jack-of-all-trades
and master of me . . .

J. W. W. returned the favor, dedicating at least one of his works to Jill Emerson.

Berkley called the book *Sensuous*. It's not a terrible title. (*I Am Curious—Thirty*, which is what they called *Thirty*—now *that's* a terrible title.) *Sensuous* is merely a pedestrian title. But I'm fairly confident the same keen mind was responsible for both of these retitlings. The first was an attempt to tie in with *I Am Curious—Yellow*, a faintly pornographic Swedish film that got a lot of press when Jackie Kennedy decked a photographer who snapped a shot of her emerging from the theater where it was shown. That made it a nine-day wonder, and a lot more than nine days had passed by the time Jill's book came out with its remarkably lame title.

And *Sensuous* was someone's way to cash in on the great success of *The Sensuous Woman*, written by Joan Garrity under the pseudonym "J" and published brilliantly by Lyle Stuart. You liked *The Sensuous Woman*? Well, here's *Sensuous*. Maybe you'll like this one, too.

Still, not a terrible title. But I like *A Madwoman's Diary* better, perhaps because I'm the one who thought it up. Or Jill did. Or maybe it was Jack Wells . . .

THIRTY

Jill Emerson was born in 1964, in Tonawanda, New York, where she wrote a sensitive novel of a young woman's emerging sexual identity as a lesbian. Midwood Tower published it as *Warm and Willing.* Later that year I moved to Racine, Wisconsin, and wouldn't you know it? Jill came along with me, and in due course Midwood published *Enough of Sorrow.* Same theme, different characters, and a dandy epigraph in the form of a poem by Mary Carolyn Davies. Another of Ms. Davies' poems is quoted in one of my Bernie Rhodenbarr books, and all of this leads me to the suspicion that Jill Emerson and I are the only persons left who could even recognize the woman's name.

Then Jill went into retirement.

It wasn't hard for her to disappear. No one but an editor or two at Midwood ever knew she existed, and they had no idea she was me. I agented those two books myself, submitting them over the transom, and some day I'll have to publish the letters Ms. Emerson and her publishers exchanged. I haven't held on to much of my correspondence, but those were keepers.

A few years later I was living on twenty-two rolling acres in West Central New Jersey, a mile from the Delaware River. There was a new frankness to be found in mainstream American fiction, and a number of prominent writers were using words and describing actions that were well beyond the pale of the old Nightstand Books /Midwood/ Beacon Books days. Berkley Books, a paperback arm of G. P. Putnam's Sons, decided that what the literary world could use was a line of candid erotic novels, and my agent, Henry Morrison, figured this would be right up my alley.

He peddled me to them as one Lawrence Josephson. I don't know how Henry picked that name but suspect he wanted to guard against the possibility of referring to me as Larry by mistake. (It is a propensity of the nonwriter, incidentally, when forced to devise an alias, to choose a first name or variant thereof as a surname. Williams, Andrews, Thomas, Davidson—

that sort of thing. Don't ask me why.) I don't know who Mr. Josephson was supposed to be, but unspecified circumstances in his life required that he employ a pen name and I told Henry I'd use the name Jill Emerson. That was OK with him, and OK with Berkley, and the first book I wrote for them was this one, which I called *Thirty*.

Around this time I was having a problem with fiction.

I wasn't having a trouble writing it, and I wasn't even having trouble selling it—although I sometimes had difficulty living on what I earned from it. No, the problem I was having was a little different.

I was having trouble believing in it.

I mean, here's this novel, any novel, and what am I to make of it? Who's telling us this story? If it's in the third person, whether single- or multiple-viewpoint, where did these words come from? What are they doing on the page?

And even if it's the most natural sort of presentation, with a first-person narrator recounting his story to me, where'd he come from and why is he nattering in my ear? And in fact it's not his voice in my ear, it's his words on the page, and how did they get there?

Yes, I know. It's a convention. In the Soviet Union, a worker explained the system thus: "We pretend to work, and they pretend to pay us." In the novel, there's a comparable mutual pretense in effect.

Still, it bothered me.

And I found myself more interested in works of fiction in which part of the premise held that they were documents. I was impressed by Sue Kaufman's *Diary of a Mad Housewife*, and Mark Harris's brilliant epistolary novel, *Wake Up, Stupid*. A couple of my novels pretended to be true-life novels authored by their protagonists, and *Such Men Are Dangerous* (by and about one Paul Kavanagh) and *No Score* (by and about Chip Harrison) are examples thereof.

Thus *Thirty*. Although this book wouldn't pretend to be other than the fictional creation of Jill Emerson, it would be written in the form of a diary.

One of the currents of thought that gave rise to *Thirty* was the notion that turning thirty was an epochal point in a woman's life, that it was some sort of line of demarcation. If nothing else, a thirtieth birthday was surely an event.

How well the book I wrote elaborated on this premise is not for me to say. But it was enough of a part of the fabric of the book so that I never doubted what I wanted to call the thing.

Thirty, of course. And the title had an extra little measure of significance. In the newspaper business, this is what you put at the end of your copy, to show that it was finished:

-30-

Now I don't know where this came from, although you can Google your way to a couple of explanations that seem at least half-plausible. Thirty—an end, a beginning, a turning point. Whatever.

Then some moron changed the title.

All right, these things happen. And in the world of paperback originals they happened rather often, and the author was rarely consulted. Often the first he knew of it was when he held a copy of the printed book in his hands.

Here's what they changed it to: *I Am Curious —Thirty*.

That makes little enough sense on the face of it, and even less when you know the reference. A year or so before the book came out, a sexually adventurous Swedish film was released in America with the English title *I Am Curious—Yellow*. That title didn't mean much of anything, as far as I can tell, although it may be just plain terrific in Swedish. But *Thirty*'s new title was designed, I guess, to make people think of this Swedish film, which by then had pretty much disappeared from this country's consciousness, not to mention its theaters.

Oh, never mind.

Jill Emerson followed *Thirty* with a book she called *Three*. That was changed to *Threesome*, which was probably an improvement, truth to tell. Next came *A Madwoman's Diary*, another shot at diary form, and that title was changed to *Sensuous*. Next came a novel in the form of letters to and from the protagonist—but so many people who read it liked it so much that I put my own name on it instead of Jill's, and sent it not to Berkley but to some hardcover publishers. Bernard Geis published it with my title: *Ronald Rabbit Is a Dirty Old Man*.

But that's another story. In fact it's a whole batch of other stories, to be recounted elsewhere.

I hope you enjoyed this one.

-30-

THREESOME

Jill Emerson's career began with a pair of lesbian novels, the first written in 1964 in an office in Tonawanda, New York, at the intersection of Colvin Boulevard and Eggert Road (where Jill got her mail), the second a year later in my home office on the second floor of a side-by-side duplex at 4051 Marquette Drive, in Racine, Wisconsin. The books are *Warm and Willing* and *Enough of Sorrow*, and they're available as ebooks. Each includes an afterword detailing how they came to be written.

Then Jill went into retirement. She emerged from it to write an erotic novel in diary form, published as a paperback original by Berkley Books. It, too, is available as an ebook—*Thirty*—with an afterword recounting, among other things, how I'd become disenchanted with the traditional form of novels and preferred that they appear to be something else, whether a diary or an exchange of letters or a manuscript found in a bottle. Something, at any rate, that kept you from wondering just who was telling you all of this, and why.

Threesome was Jill's second book for Berkley, and I can't begin to tell you how much enjoyment I got out of writing it. It was very much a tour de force, and the tour was a pleasure.

The idea grew out of a recent publishing phenomenon. *Naked Came the Stranger* was the product of a batch of journalists—all of them connected with *Long Island Newsday*, if I remember correctly. They took turns writing chapters of a trashy novel, got somebody's girlfriend to lend them her bare behind for the cover photo—it was a splendid behind, I must say—and promoted the resulting product artfully enough to get on the bestseller list.

God knows they weren't the first to think of this idea. In point of fact, five friends and I had the idea of producing a book in a single night, with each one taking a turn writing a chapter while the other five played poker downstairs. (I recount this in detail in the introduction to my memoir, *Step by Step*. It, uh, didn't work, but it's failure was quite spectacular.) We never had bestseller dreams for *Lust Fuck*, and it's just as well. But it worked out for the *Newsday* crowd, and it's been tried occasionally since then, some times successfully, sometimes not.

But for *Threesome* what I dreamed up was this: Three people, a man and two women who've established a sexual ménage à trois, are themselves inspired by the success of *Naked Came the Stranger*, decide that they ought to write a book in the same fashion. And what better subject could they conceive than their own relationship and its evolution? So they agree that they'll take turns writing chapters, and what we're reading are the chapters that they write.

But as each writes a chapter, and as each reads the chapters the others have written, they begin to discover things they hadn't known. And what they read affects what they write, and their life together continues to evolve. There's not only the story of What Happened before they started writing the book, there's the story of What Happens as they write it.

Damn, it was fun.

I wrote the book in New York, at the Hotel Royalton on West Forty-fourth Street. The hotel's still there, but it's now a trendy and pricey place. When I went there it was owned by two brothers, Henry and Barry Shenk; the same three doormen traded shifts there for thirty years. I could get a room there for ten bucks a night, and they may have given me a weekly rate.

It was while I was writing *Threesome* that I had an experience that I wound up adapting some months later, in a book called *Ronald Rabbit Is a Dirty Old Man*. I was done with the day's work and went down to the Village, where I wound up drinking in the Kettle of Fish on Macdougal Street. (It's not there anymore. It closed and reappeared on West Third Street, and closed again, and blossomed yet again on Christopher Street, where the Lion's Head pub used to be.)

I had a lot to drink and came out of there just as a great big station wagon full of girls pulled up in front, with their teacher at the wheel. They were from a fancy Catholic girls' school in Connecticut, and they thought I was exotic and worth cultivating, and I got in the car and went back to Connecticut with them.

Where do you get your ideas, Mr. Block? Oh, I dunno, they just sort of pop into my head.

When this happens to Laurence Clarke, the hero of *Ronald Rabbit*, he gets lucky with all six of them. That's the neat thing about fiction, you get to make it come out right. I made out a wee bit with one of the girls—well, maybe it was with two of them—but it didn't go all that far.

The next day I went back to the Royalton and resumed work on *Threesome*.

Where do you get your ideas, Mr. Block? Oh, I dunno, they just sort of pop into my head.

THE TROUBLE WITH EDEN

In late 1968 or early 1969, I moved with my wife and daughters from a house in the center of New Brunswick, New Jersey, to an eighteenth century farmhouse on twelve rolling acres a mile from the Delaware River. We kept a variety of animals and grew things in the garden, and this was as I'd expected. But there were two things I did not anticipate. One was that I would have to go away from there, all the way back to New York City, to get any work done. The other was that I'd open an art gallery to give myself something to do in my rural paradise.

The art gallery was in New Hope, Pennsylvania, right across the river from Lambertville. New Hope, in Bucks County, had had a reputation as an artists' colony for a few generations and boasted a little theater and a batch of art galleries, along with bookstores and antique dealers and cute little shops to sell cute little things to tourists, most of whom were neither cute nor little.

I found a store for rent in an enclosed shopping mall and signed a year's lease. I'm damned if I know what led me to think this was a good idea. I knew a batch of artists and figured I could get them to give me things to hang on the walls, and—oh, never mind. Nowadays it's hard to get me to go see a movie or buy a new shirt, but back then I'd embark on the wildest kind of adventure on not much more than a whim.

I knew nothing about business, but that was okay, because the gallery didn't do any. Whenever I went into the city to write a book, I closed up shop while I was gone. When I was home, I'd open up and sit there until it was time to go across the street and have a drink at the Logan Inn. That was the best part of the operation, that and hanging out with Jim and Flory Toney, who did my custom framing whenever I managed to sell something.

After a year, my lease was up and I was out of there. It was a learning experience, and I learned not to make that particular mistake again. And I did meet some interesting people, and hear some interesting stories.

And, when it came time to write a big trashy commercial novel, I knew right where to set it.

By this time I'd written three erotic novels for Berkley Books as Jill Emerson; a fourth, *Ronald Rabbit Is a Dirty Old Man*, wound up in hardcover with Bernard Geis. Now I don't know who thought that Jill ought to write a big, juicy, trashy *Peyton Place*–type of book, but Henry brought the idea to me, and I thought Bucks County would provide a good setting.

The deal was an attractive one, with a hefty advance. Berkley was a division of G. P. Putnam's Sons, and the deal was hard/soft; the book would be first a Berkley hardcover, then a paperback.

I wrote most of it in an apartment at 235 West End Avenue. When we first moved to the country, and I found I couldn't get any writing done there, I went into the city, took a room at the Hotel Royalton—then a modestly priced family-run establishment, before some genius took it over and tarted it up—and wrote a book in a week. Soon after that I leased a studio apartment on West Thirty-fifth Street, and then Brian Garfield and I took a place together, holding a weekly poker game there, staying over whenever one or the other of us had a late night in the city, and getting some writing done. I believe Brian wrote most of *Kolchak's Gold* there. I wrote a batch of things, too, and one of them was *The Trouble with Eden*.

Some of the characters were based to one degree or another on some of the people I'd known in and around New Hope, and one at least recognized himself. He was an actor and a partner in the mall bookstore, and he did in fact greatly resemble Benjamin Franklin. "Larry put me in a book," he told people. "But he's made me bisexual, for God's sake, and *everybody* knows I'm a plain and simple faggot. Do you think I could sue his publisher? Would I get anything, do you suppose? And would the publicity be good for the book? Because I wouldn't want to do it if it would get Larry in any kind of trouble . . ."

Well, he didn't sue, which was probably just as well. Would the publicity of a lawsuit have helped? I don't think anything would have helped. Berkley had commissioned the book with the intention of making a big fat bestseller out of it, but they never put any muscle into it and didn't sell many copies.

There'd been a big fat bestseller a few years earlier called *The Devil in Bucks County*, and I'm sure the Berkley folks were aware of it. They probably had it in mind when they made the deal. The title I suggested was *The Trouble with Bucks County*, and they used half of it. *The Trouble with Eden*—well, it's not a bad title.

Reviewers overlooked it completely as far as I can tell, with a single curious exception. In a long article about books in *Esquire*, a reviewer whose name I've long since forgotten launched into a discussion of a book that he (or maybe she) had picked up a week ago without great expectations. It looked like trash but turned out to be far more gripping and involving than he or she anticipated. Well-wrought characters, interesting plot developments—really pretty good.

And then suddenly the review hung a U-turn, and its author said that further on the book turned out to be trash after all and, on balance, a big disappointment. I'll tell you, it was as though the reviewer read half the book, wrote half the review, ate something that turned his stomach, finished the book, and went on to finish the review. I can't say I minded—it was, as they say at the Oscars, victory enough merely to be nominated—and I can't say I disagreed with its conclusion. But it was damn strange.

Ah well. It's probably not a good book, but I have a warm spot for *Eden*. Like the curate's egg, I think parts of it are very good indeed.

A WEEK AS ANDREA BENSTOCK

Athena, goddess of wisdom, emerged full-blown from the head of Zeus. Jill Emerson sprang similarly from my own self, but whether from the head or some lower organ is a matter of some speculation.

The woman has had a checkered career. Her first two novels, *Warm and Willing* and *Enough of Sorrow*, are sensitive fictional explorations of the lesbian demimonde of their day. A few years later she wrote three distinctly erotic novels, *Thirty*, *Threesome*, and *A Madwoman's Diary*. She followed with a fat *Peyton Place*-type book, *The Trouble with Eden*. And then she published *A Week as Andrea Benstock*.

It was clearly her most ambitious work, and her most successful. And, at least so far, it's her last appearance in print.

I can trace the origin of *A Week as Andrea Benstock* to two distinct sources. The first inspired my attempting the book, while the second inspired its form.

Let me consider the second first. In 1949, the Belgian author Georges Simenon published a novel called—well, who knows what he called it, but the English translation bore the title—*Four Days in a Lifetime*. I must have read it sometime in the late 1950s because what I recall of the experience is that I was in my parents' house on Starin Avenue at the time.

Besides its title, all I remember of the book is its structure. It consisted of four parts, each taking place entirely within a single day of its protagonist's life. And those four days were all you needed. They gave you the full picture of the man's existence . . . or, at least, all Simenon felt like giving you.

I thought it was brilliant, and the device—if not the plot or characters—stayed in my mind.

If Simenon gave me the structure of *Andrea Benstock*, a woman named Peggy Roth pointed me at the book's subject matter and at the same time made me believe I was good enough to write it.

Peggy was a highly placed editor at Dell Publishing—editor in chief, if I remember correctly. My own editor there, Bill Grose, reported to her, and on one occasion in the early 1970s the three of us had lunch together. I'd written a batch of sex fact books that Dell had published (sexual case histories, truth to tell) and would soon begin the Matthew Scudder series there, but at the time I don't believe Dell had published any of my fiction. I don't remember much about our lunch except that it was typical of publisher lunches of the time in that we all had a lot to drink. The conversation wandered all over the place, and at one point Peggy asked me who my favorite writer was. I replied (and would very likely still reply) that it was John O'Hara.

"Oh, you're a much better writer than he ever was," Peggy Roth said.

Now that could only have been the martinis talking, and I'm sure I knew it at the time and surely know it now. She couldn't possibly have believed it, and if she did, well, she was wrong.

But her words, even if I recognized them as outrageous and alcohol-driven, nevertheless allowed me to believe that I might try to play in that league. I'd never get a Golden Glove or hit for the circuit, but I might be able to sit on the bench. Maybe pitch batting practice, say.

Then Peggy asked me about my background, and I said I'd grown up in a middle-class Jewish family in Buffalo, New York. "Then that's what you should write about," she said.

I don't think it had ever occurred to me that anyone would want to read a novel with such a setting or that I would ever want to write one. But Peggy Roth, a perceptive and intelligent woman, thought that was what I should write. That didn't send me rushing to my desk, but it was something to think about.

I don't remember when it all came together, but eventually I found I had a book in mind. Like Simenon's novel, it would consist of scattered days in a life—not four but seven of them, the titular week in the protagonist's life. And they'd be strewn over a decade, beginning with her wedding, when she takes her husband's name and becomes Andrea Benstock. The days chosen wouldn't necessarily be the days on which major events in her life happened but would rather be representative days. And there'd be no elaborate recapitulation of what had transpired in the months and years between one day and the next; we'd get that information, but only insofar as it would be apt to come to her mind at each present moment.

I don't keep journals, so I can't say just when I started work on the book or even when I finished it. It took a while. Because of its utterly episodic structure, it was easy to put it aside between sections and turn to something else, something with the promise of immediate income. I was married to my first wife when I began the book, and that marriage ended in the summer of 1973.

I moved into a studio apartment on West Fifty-eighth Street, and that same year Peggy Roth took ill and died far too young of pneumonia. When I finished the book, she was one of its two dedicatees; the other was my stepfather, Joe Rosenberg.

My agent, Henry Morrison, sent the book around. I don't know if Arbor House was the first place he sent it, but that's where it landed; Donald I. Fine, who had created Arbor House, wanted to meet the writer and was surprised when Jill Emerson turned out to be a man.

He wanted me to use my own name on it. He felt strongly about it—Don was a man who felt strongly about most things, if he felt about them at all—but I was adamant that I wanted the book to have Jill's name on it. We each had reasons for our feelings. Don believed, and you can make of this what you will, that a novel would be taken more seriously if a man wrote it. I believed that a novel told from a woman's viewpoint would receive a warmer reception if a woman were its author.

Who was right? Damned if I know. He could point to George Eliot, I suppose, and *Madame Bovary*. I would probably find someone to point to, if I worked at it. One thing we both agreed on was that it was my call, and I didn't waver. The book was published in 1975 as *A Week as Andrea Benstock*, by Jill Emerson.

Don was good at whipping up enthusiasm for subsidiary rights sales, and he did a couple of good things for *Andrea Benstock*. The novel was serialized in *Redbook* and paperback rights went to Ballantine Books. He was famous for getting book club sales, but I don't believe he managed that this time.

I would have told you then, and would have believed it myself, that I wanted a pen name for sound commercial reasons. And I may have had commercial reasons, and they may or may not have been sound, but hindsight lets me see they were largely beside the point.

I'd never really used Buffalo as a background before— except as a setting for genre fiction that might as easily have taken place in Butte, Montana, or Boca Raton, Florida. Nor had I ever written about Jews, except as some minor characters here and there were so designated. But *Andrea Benstock* was set specifically in the Jewish community of Buffalo. It was by no means a roman à clef, none of these people were even loosely based on real Buffalonians, or real Jews. But it was my own background I was drawing upon, and that was much closer to the bone of personal inner and outer experience than I was inclined to go. So when I used that background, I made the character—and author—a woman.

Andrea's surname, by the way, was that of a family I knew in Buffalo: Mel and Pearl and their daughter, Marcy. None of them had any further connection to the book or to any of its characters. I just liked the name. Andrea Benstock—I *still* like the name.

Sheldon Lord and Andrew Shaw Novels

69 BARROW STREET

Ah yes. Barrow Street.

I was born in Buffalo, at the other end of the state, and my first visit to New York City came ten and a half years later, in December of 1948. My father and I rode the Empire State Limited to Grand Central and stayed for three or four nights at the Hotel Commodore, right next door to the train station. We found time to visit an aunt and uncle of his, but most of the weekend was devoted to showing me New York, and we didn't miss much. We rode the Third Avenue el down to the Bowery, where I saw a man emerge from a saloon, scream at the top of his lungs, then turn around and go back in again. We rode the ferry to Bedloes Island—since renamed Liberty Island—and saw the statue. We went to the top of the Empire State Building. We saw a Broadway show—*Where's Charley?* with Ray Bolger—and the live telecast of *Toast of the Town,* which was what Ed Sullivan's show was called back in the day. (At the time, I'd not yet seen a TV set; I found the monitor more fascinating than what was occurring onstage.)

I must have known then that I'd wind up in New York.

There was another visit a couple of years later, with my mother and sister along this time, and all four of us stayed at the Commodore. We saw *South Pacific* this time. I don't remember where else we went, or what else we did, but one place I'm sure we didn't get was Greenwich Village. I never got to the Village until the summer of 1956, when I lived there.

I went to Antioch College, in Yellow Springs, Ohio. There were a lot of things that set the school apart, but its defining element was a program of cooperative education. Students spent half the year on campus, the other half out in the world, acquiring vocational and life experience in an appropriate short-term job. Like many of my classmates, I spent my whole freshman year in Yellow Springs, and in August of 1956 I went off to New York to begin my first co-op job, as a mail boy at Pines Publications. I got there as I'd done the first time, on the Empire State Limited, and met Paul Grillo right there in the terminal, in front of the big clock. He'd been my hall advisor during the academic year, and now we'd be rooming together. He'd already found us a place, and told me how to get there—147 West Fourteenth Street, and I was to take the shuttle to Times Square and the IRT downtown to Fourteenth Street.

That first night, I went out exploring, and I managed to find my way to a jazz club that had come well recommended by my roommate, Steve Schwerner. It was the Café Bohemia, at 15 Barrow Street, and I stood at the bar and had a drink and listened to Al Cohn and Zoot Sims.

I explored some more over the weekend. A fellow I'd met a summer earlier when we'd both worked at Camp Lakeland lived on Bleecker Street, and introduced me to Caricatures, a coffee house on Macdougal with a batch of caricatures in the window, alone with a signed note from Maxwell Bodenheim, the archetypical Village bohemian who'd been murdered a few years earlier. The place was owned and run by a woman named Liz, who was more interested in her ongoing bridge game in the back room than in the customers out front. But she did serve cheeseburgers on toasted rye bread, and they were outstanding.

Monday morning I reported to work at Pines Publications. And by the beginning of September Paul Grillo and I, along with Fred Anliot, had moved south to 108 West Twelfth Street, and south and west to 54 Barrow Street.

Where I spent the months of September and October, until it was time to return to Yellow Springs.

That was a wonderful apartment, parlor floor front, the living room fronting on Barrow Street, a bedroom at the rear, a kitchen–dining room in between. I wrote a story there called "You Can't Lose," and it eventually became my first sale when *Manhunt* bought it a year later. I got friendly with the folk music enthusiasts who spent Sunday afternoons around the circle in Washington Square, and when the cops cleared the area at six o'clock, the party would move on to our place on Barrow Street.

When October ended and it was time to return to Yellow Springs, we passed the apartment to a couple of other Antiochians, and they kept it for the next three months. It may have stayed in Antioch hands for another semester, or maybe not, but eventually it went back to the landlord. Now I suppose it's a co-op, or a condo; if it's still a rental, it probably runs to $2,500 a month. We paid $90, split three ways. Then again, I was earning $40 a week at Pines Publications, and taking home $34. All things in proportion.

It was two summers later, in August of 1958, that Sheldon Lord wrote his first novel. The book was called *Carla,* and was both set and written in Buffalo. I'd dropped out of Antioch after my second year, when I'd lucked into a job as an editor at a literary agency. I kept that job for the better part of a year, then went home to Buffalo and wrote a novel (*Strange Are the Ways of Love,* by Lesley Evans), and got an assignment from my former employer to write an erotic novel for a new publisher, Midwood Tower Books, the creation of one Harry Shorten. I wrote the book, Harry loved it, and Sheldon Lord was in business.

Sheldon Lord's second book was *A Strange Kind of Love,* and it seems to me *69 Barrow Street* was third, but I may be wrong about that. I was back in Yellow Springs when I wrote *A Strange Kind of Love,* and I wrote *Born to Be Bad* there as well, and it seems to me *69 Barrow Street* came between the two.

But who cares?

I liked the idea of a book set in a single building, and telling the stories of its various inhabitants. And I wanted to use the Village in a book, and what better street than Barrow Street? Harold Robbins, who'd written a terrific realistic novel in *A Stone for Danny Fisher,* had followed it with some less terrific but soundly commercial books, and one of them was indeed set in a single building, and the title was *79 Park Avenue.* Why not improve in that a wee bit by reducing the number by ten? Call the book *69 Barrow Street*—an address which doesn't actually exist, incidentally, so don't go looking for it—and I'd give the book a clearly sexual tag while doing absolutely nothing censorable, *Hey, it's an address, it's a fucking number, and what the matter with that?*

It was such a brilliant idea that I wondered how come Harold Robbins hadn't thought of it first. And, years later, I found out that he had. It had been his original intention to call his book *69 Park Avenue,* and that was the title he'd attached to the manuscript when he sent it to his publisher.

But cooler heads prevailed.

As they sometimes do. Fortunately there were no cooler heads in Harry Shorten's offices, and my title stayed.

Ages and ages ago, that was. I don't know that I expected to be around so many years later, but I'll tell you this: I never thought for a moment that Sheldon Lord would still be with us, or that anyone on earth would actually be reading *69 Barrow Street* in a year starting with a 2. I'm damn glad that I'm still around, and, yes, glad to say the same for Sheldon Lord, and this creation of his.

Hope you enjoyed it.

APRIL NORTH

April North was the first book I wrote for Beacon Books, although it may or may not have been the first title of mine that they published. *A Diet of Treacle* (which Beacon called *Pads Are for Passion*) was also published in 1961 and went to Beacon after several other publishers had passed it up. I don't know the order in which they were published, and, now that I think about it, I can't imagine why anyone would care.

I can't say I remember much about the writing of *April North.* Now I have a copy in front of me as I write these lines and I could read it and refresh my memory, but I'm not going to do that. I mean, I wrote it. Why would I want to read it?

That reminds me of a story. Some years ago, a book tour led me to the Left Coast Crime Conference, held that year in Scottsdale, Arizona. Robert B. Parker was also in attendance, and I sat in on a program in which he fielded questions from the audience. Bob didn't much like to give speeches but was comfortable with a Q&A, and he charmed his audience as effortlessly as his hero Spenser charmed them in print.

One of the questions concerned Bob's view of his own work. What was his favorite Spenser novel?

"Oh, hell, I don't know," he said. "I let go of them once I write them. I never read them once they're published. Does anybody?" He'd evidently spotted me in the rear of the hall, and called out, "Larry, do you ever read your own work?"

"I read nothing else," I replied.

Well, it got a good laugh. In point of fact I do sometimes reread books of mine. But I find it virtually impossible to look over my very early work. I'm not sure what it is that puts me off. It may be that my writing ability has—thank God!—increased over time, and that the work of my less skillful earlier self seems amateurish, clumsy, and wooden. It seems just as likely that it's the young author I don't want to look at, that the glimpses of my younger self that the work affords embarrass me with revelations of callowness and vapidity. Or perhaps I'm just afraid to open those several closets for fear of what I might find there.

Never mind. I'm not going to reread *April North* just so I can natter on about it to you. I mean, you've already read the book. And it's not *Finnegan's Wake*. You don't need to have me explain it to you.

Which won't put me at a loss for words.

You know what I've always liked about *April North?*

The title.

Which is to say that I like the protagonist's name. Beacon must have liked it, too, because the company didn't change the title. As a publisher, the company could be a pain in the ass, not so much because their editors changed titles but because they were apt to change everything else. A team of editorial hirelings went through every manuscript Beacon bought, and if they didn't make changes on just about every page—just arbitrary rewording to no apparent purpose—then they weren't doing what they'd been hired to do and risked losing their jobs. But I didn't realize they were doing this until I'd already published three books with them and had moved on to other things.

One thing we agreed on, though, was the title. I still like it. It sounds, I dunno, classy. And I came up with it while trying to work a variation on a theme.

My friend and colleague Hal Dresner wrote several books for Nightstand Books as Don Holliday. (Only a few, after which he leased the name to ghostwriters.) One of the ones he wrote and showed to me featured a blowsy dame whom he called June East—as a play on Mae West.

Hence April North, who had nothing else in common with either June East or Mae West. But I have to say I still like her name better than either of theirs.

The other thing I can tell you about *April North*—still without my having to read it—is that because of it I was threatened with a lawsuit.

By this time—late 1962, early 1963—I'd moved back from New York City to Buffalo, or more specifically to 48 Ebling Avenue, in the township of Tonawanda. The house had a full finished basement attractively paneled in knotty cedar, and I'd tricked out an alcove down there as an office where I wrote a little of this and a little of that, but nothing at all for Beacon. A couple of other writers were playing Sheldon Lord for me, and in return for the entrée my name afforded to Beacon Books, I was getting a little off the top. Two hundred dollars a book, if memory serves.

My agent found these writers. I never knew who they were and I'm not sure they knew who I was. But one fellow who ghosted one or two books for me was my friend Peter Hochstein, who had been my occasional college roommate. He was between jobs in the advertising business, which he professed to loathe, so he set up shop in a hotel on Broadway and Sixty-ninth Street and knocked out a couple of books as Sheldon Lord. Then he decided he missed office life and gabbing at the water cooler, and went back to Madison Avenue.

But in the interim he did one thing he wasn't supposed to do, which was tell the world about our ghostwriting deal. The word got around to Antioch College in Yellow Springs, Ohio, where we had both gone to school and where *April North* is essentially set. (The town in the book is given as Antrim and Yellow Springs is mentioned as being nearby, but although Antrim's fictional, it might as well be Yellow Springs.)

Well. There's a character in the book called Danny Duncan. And in Yellow Springs a Martha Duncan learned of the book, got hold of a copy, and was outraged that her son's name had been used in the book. Now I didn't know Martha Duncan, or Danny Duncan, either. I'd once met a Judy Duncan, who turned out to be Martha's daughter, but the meeting was brief and unmemorable—I think I sold her a guitar—and I didn't know she had a brother or a mother or, really, anything in the world but a thirdhand guitar.

But evidently Peter had known Martha Duncan, although not all that well, just well enough that Martha felt betrayed because Peter had gone and put her son in a book—and a marginally obscene book at that. So she wrote a letter to Peter, whom she of course believed to be the book's author, and she sent a copy of that letter, along with a letter from her lawyer, to the folks at Beacon.

Who sent the letter to my agent, who sent it to me.

I was rattled. What concerned me most was that Beacon would now know that I'd run in a ghost. That knowledge, plus the threat of a lawsuit, might well prompt them to wash their hands of Sheldon Lord altogether. I wrote to Martha Duncan at length, telling her that I'd written the book myself, and that I didn't know her or her son, and that the description of the book's Danny Duncan ("a tall rangy senior who played first base on the baseball team and second-string end on the football team") didn't seem libelous to me.

I probably pointed out that the book was published in 1961, when Peter was still finishing up at Antioch and her son had not yet become either tall or rangy. In any event, I heard nothing further of or from Martha Duncan. And, mirabile dictu, my relationship with Beacon remained as it had been, with various ghosts writing various books. When they did, I got my two hundred dollars.

I still like the title.

CAMPUS TRAMP

In June of 1955 I graduated from Bennett High School in Buffalo, New York. The school was named after one Lewis J. Bennett, and you now know as much about the man as I ever

did. Having one's name on something enduring—a school, a
bridge, a building—is thought to provide immortality of a sort,
but if that's immortality, well, I'm with the Persian philosopher
Omar Khayyam, "take the cash and let the credit go." What's
the big deal about having your name bandied about by people
who haven't got a clue who you were?

But I digress.

After I graduated from Bennett, I spent the summer as a
counselor-in-training at nearby Camp Lakeland. In September I
arrived at Antioch College in Yellow Springs, Ohio. My parents
had both graduated from Cornell University, as had my mother's
brothers, and it had been taken for granted that I would follow
in their wake. But sometime in my junior year my parents had
heard about Antioch, where the son of a friend of a friend had
gone, and decided it was just the thing for their son. Antioch's
most striking feature was its co-op plan, whereby students
were placed in jobs designed to give them genuine vocational
experience for half of each year. My parents liked that, and they
also learned that Antioch was a refuge for the quirky and the
unconventional, and that sounded about right for young Larry.

The summer before my senior year, we visited the campus on
the way home from a Florida vacation. I seem to recall a student
showing us around, pointing out buildings like a hunting dog
pointing out game birds. Did it make an impression? Not that I
recall. My parents thought I should apply there, so I did. They
thought I should apply to Cornell as well, so I did that, too. I
was a pretty suggestible kid, and inclined to do as I was told.

All of that changed, but never mind.

I was accepted at both schools, and I learned I'd get a nice
scholarship to Cornell, having scored high on the New York
State scholarship exam. My folks sent me to Antioch anyway

and not without financial sacrifice. They really thought it would be good for me, and, looking back, I guess it was.

I spent the whole of my freshman year on campus in Yellow Springs, as did a substantial percentage of entering students. I had known for a couple of years that I was going to become a writer, and I wrote some poems and short stories. I submitted them to magazines with no real hope of success and regarded the inevitable rejection slips as badges of honor and ample compensation for my efforts. I displayed them with some pride on my dorm room wall.

The school year ran through June, and come August I was in New York, living in Greenwich Village and working in the mail room at Pines Publications, a diverse publisher of paperbacks and magazines. I returned to Antioch for the fall semester, spent the winter job period working in Buffalo at the Erie County Comptroller's Office, went back to Antioch for the spring term, and then arranged that my next job would be my Own Plans. I went home, bought an aging Buick, and drove it to Cape Cod, Massachusetts, where I intended to get a subsistence job and write stories. I'd almost sold a story that I'd written while living in the Village, and figured I could rewrite it and sell it, and write other things and sell them, too.

I got a room in an attic and wrote a batch of stories, but the Cape didn't work out too well, and I wound up in New York. I went to an employment agency, took a blind test, and landed a job as an editor at a literary agency. Every day I would read a batch of stories submitted, with fees, by what the world had not yet learned to call wannabes. It was my task to write them lengthy letters assuring them that they were supremely talented (they were not), that it was the plot structure of their stories that was at fault (that was the least of it), and that we would welcome further submissions from them, with further fees. (That last, I must say, was the truth.)

It was purely wonderful experience, the best possible training for a writer, and I could see right away that this was not a job I wanted to abandon at the end of a three-month Antioch job period. Besides, I'd sold the story I revised on the Cape, and had every reason to assume I'd sell more, now that I was working for a literary agent. So I dropped out of Antioch and kept the job.

If it was too good to give up after three months, it wasn't so great that I wanted to hang on to it for more than a year. I resigned at the end of the spring of 1958, went back to Buffalo, wrote a sensitive lesbian novel in a couple of weeks, sent it to my agent, and went off to Mexico with my buddy Steve Schwerner. We came back sooner than we'd planned, and, on the strength of that lesbian novel, I got an assignment from my agent to do a book for Midwood Tower, a new firm under the aegis of one Harry Shorten, devoted to the publication of sexy paperbacks.

I wrote a book called *Carla*, and it was catnip to Harry Shorten. There was one scene in which the titular heroine (and that's the right adjective, trust me) has it off with a gas pump jockey in the service station's grease pit, and Harry thought that scene was the cat's pajamas. It blew him away, so to speak, and he wanted more.

Meanwhile, I'd made arrangements to return to Antioch, where I'd spend the fall quarter taking classes, the winter quarter editing the school newspaper, and the spring back in class again.

Well, here's the question: How are you gonna keep 'em down on the farm after they've seen Paree? All I wanted to do, really, was write books and stories. And I'd sold upwards of a dozen stories to the crime fiction magazines, and some articles to men's magazines, and a little of this and a little of that elsewhere. Harry

Shorten wanted more books from me, and the first house that got a look at that lesbian novel, Fawcett Crest, wanted to publish it. So I could write books and stories and actually get paid for them, or I could read Henry Fielding and Tobias Smollett and write papers on the Eighteenth Century English Novel.

Well, what do you think happened?

I got through the year, but don't ask me how. I did try to drop out during the fall but was persuaded to change my mind. I edited the *Antioch Record* winter quarter, and that went okay, but during the two academic terms I did not exactly cover myself with glory.

Then summer came, and I couldn't find a co-op job that I liked, and I don't suppose I looked very hard for one. I arranged to go on my Own Plans again and moved to New York, where I took a room at the Hotel Rio on West Forty-seventh Street and began writing books.

The first was *Campus Tramp.*

You were probably wondering if I'd ever get to it, and so was I. But here we are, in July of 1959, and there I was, in my room at the Rio, typing furiously. By this time I'd written and sold four books—*Strange Are the Ways of Love*, published by Crest Books under the name of Lesley Evans, and three novels published by Midwood under the name Sheldon Lord, *Carla* (which I wrote in Buffalo) and two books I knocked off during that year at Antioch, *A Strange Kind of Love* and *Born to be Bad.*

Now my agent informed me that a new publisher, Bill Hamling, was starting a company to be called Nightstand Books, and that I'd been chosen to write for them. Midwood had been paying me six hundred dollars a book, and Hamling would pay seven hundred fifty dollars.

I decided a college novel might be just the ticket. I'd been trying to figure out what to try for Fawcett/Crest—after all, they had paid me two thousand dollars for that lesbian novel. But on some level I didn't really believe I was good enough to write for that good a house, and that self-doubt kept me from trying. I'd been thinking my second book for Crest might be set on a campus, and when Nightstand came along I took that idea and aimed it at them.

I wrote *Campus Tramp* in a couple of weeks.

The only college with which I was familiar was Antioch, so it was an easy decision to set the book there—or at its fictional equivalent, which I called Clifton. And, to amuse myself and any other Antiochian who might read the thing, I gave every character in the book the name of an actual Antioch dormitory as a surname. Since most of the dorms were named after people, guaranteeing them the immortality of, say, Lewis J. Bennett, it wasn't a stretch to fasten their names to human beings, albeit fictional ones. While I was at it, I named the buildings on Clifton's campus after some Antioch people.

I finished the book, walked a block and a half to Fifth Avenue, and turned in the manuscript to my agent, who dutifully sent it to Hamling, who thought it was just fine, even if it didn't have anybody screwing in a grease pit. I was invited to pick a new pen name and chose Andrew Shaw. Mr. Shaw now had an assignment to produce regularly for Nightstand, even as Mr. Lord was still very much in demand at Midwood. The only place that didn't want me, it turned out, was Antioch.

It was not long after I turned in *Campus Tramp* and started another writing project that a letter from Antioch's Student Personnel Committee reached me at the Rio, informing me that a review of my performance the preceding year left them with the sense that I might be happier elsewhere.

I thought that was damned perceptive of them. I would

indeed be happier elsewhere, no question about it, and wasn't it considerate of them to point that out to me? I'd already tried to drop out once and had been talked out of it by my parents, but now I had the perfect excuse. I'd been, as the British say, sent down. (It sounds much nicer than expelled, doesn't it?) And, having been sent down, I could stay down. I was free.

I think—and thought at the time—that I could have talked my way back in. The tone of the letter suggested as much. But why would I want to do that? I had books to write.

And then a curious thing happened. *Campus Tramp* was published, and word got around Yellow Springs that it was my revenge on the school, that I'd savaged the place as a way of getting even.

Getting even for what, for God's sake? For expelling me? That was the nicest thing anyone had ever done for me. For schooling me for several years? I can't think where I might have more enjoyably or profitably spent those particular years. I had no quarrel with the place, and if it was anything vis-à-vis Antioch, the book was a wink and a nod, a veritable homage.

Besides, when I wrote it I still fully expected to return to Yellow Springs in the fall. I had a year to go, and then I was scheduled to graduate. I didn't much want to go back, but I'd planned to do it anyway, so I certainly didn't think of myself as burning any bridges with *Campus Tramp*.

Go figure.

Over the years, the story of Linda Shepard became a part of campus folklore. I've heard of copies commanding unlikely prices at Senior Sales. A young woman I know—she's since become a Facebook friend—has been known to give dramatic readings at alumni gatherings.

Nightstand reissued the book a few times over the years, in one instance doing the curious task of un-Bowdlerizing it— some poor schnook of an editor went through it and added dirty words, in recognition of looser standards in the industry. Consider this schlepper whenever you start to think you have the worst job in the world.

I never thought *Campus Tramp* would be around in the present century, and never thought I'd want to allow it to happen—or to put my own name on it. But when Creeping Hemlock Press proposed a handsome new edition, how could I say no?

After all, I wrote it. And I'm never going to have my name on a high school, or a bridge, or even a public toilet, so I have to take my Lewis J. Bennett–style immortality where I find it. Remarkably, I find I'm out-and-out delighted that it's now available as an ebook. An old friend from—yes, Bennett High— recently emailed me to say he'd read and enjoyed *Campus Tramp*, and somehow found elements to praise therein. And praise, like immortality, I'll take where I find it. Why not?

CANDY

Candy, published toward the end of 1960, may have been Sheldon Lord's last book for Midwood Tower. (It wasn't the last book by Sheldon Lord—several ghostwriters produced a string of books for Beacon Books, and the last that Beacon printed was, in fact, one I wrote myself, a crime novel they called *The Sex Shuffle*, now available under my own name as *Lucky at Cards*. Nor was *Candy* the last book I wrote for Midwood; they published Jill Emerson's first two ventures in lesbian fiction, *Warm and Willing* and *Enough of Sorrow*.)

If *Candy* was my final Sheldon Lord for Harry Shorten at Midwood, I suppose there must have been eight or ten before it. And that, it seemed to me, was enough labor in that particular vineyard. I'd welcomed the assignments and had a good enough time turning out soft-core erotica, but it wasn't how I wanted to spend my writing life. It was very much my intention to write books that might be a source of satisfaction and even pride, and that was generically impossible in the field where Sheldon Lord had been making a name for himself.

I remember having read an article in which crime fiction writer Bill Gault talked about his own literary ambitions. Early on, he said, he'd wanted to become a second Ernest Hemingway, but over time he decided he was better off trying to become the best possible William Campbell Gault. While my earliest fantasies might have shown me as a second John O'Hara or James T. Farrell or John Steinbeck or Thomas Wolfe, I'd since lowered my sights, and becoming the best possible Lawrence Block seemed reasonable.

But I wasn't entirely sure what that might mean, or how to get there. Mystery fiction, it seemed to me, was both respectable and attainable, and my inner self seemed to come up with ideas that lent themselves to the genre. My first sales were short stories to crime fiction magazines, and I'd sold a couple of crime novels to Gold Medal Books by the time I wrote *Candy*.

There were times when the two genres overlapped, at least in my house. *Grifter's Game* started out as a book for Shorten; a couple of chapters in I decided it was cut out for better things and finished it accordingly. Knox Burger bought it at Gold Medal. And sometimes the reverse happened: *Cinderella Sims* was supposed to be a Gold Medal crime novel, but something went awry and I lost confidence in the book and finished it up for Bill Hamling's Nightstand Books. (*$20 Lust*, they called it, by Andrew Shaw; it's since been republished under my name and original title.)

This sort of migration, from crime to erotica or erotica to crime, isn't all that remarkable. It was perfectly reasonable for crime novels to have sex in them, and it was a fairly standard ingredient in the paperback originals Gold Medal published. And crime was no stranger to the field of erotic fiction, serving the useful function of endowing the books with at least the minimal illusion of a plot.

Candy wound up being very much a crime novel. There are two murders in it, which would seem to satisfy the genre's entrance requirements. But it never occurred to me to aim it higher than Midwood Tower, and all these years later—fifty of them, astonishingly—I have to wonder why.

It's hard to know, but I suspect I'd written a substantial amount of the book before the crime element entered the picture. I'd have had to go back and change a lot of what I'd written if I were to aim the book at a higher market, and it would have been ever so much easier to wrap it up and save any ambition for another book.

For all the books I wrote for him, I met Harry Shorten only once.

This was very much in keeping with the Scott Meredith Literary Agency's view of the author-publisher relationship. Scott didn't believe in keeping writers and publishers at arm's length—because that was far closer than he wanted them to get to one another. It was best, as he saw it, that they never meet, and just as well if they never exchanged letters or phone calls, either. The less contact writers and publishers had, the more indispensable was the agent who had established himself as their sole point of contact.

I don't know how many books I wrote for Bill Hamling. Dozens, certainly, plus dozens more ghostwritten under my name. I never did meet the man, and the only time we were in contact was when I wrote him a letter after Scott and I had ended our author-agent relationship. I had begun a book for Nightstand, which I could no longer submit as the market was a closed shop, and I wrote to find out if I could, in fact, finish this book for him. He called Scott, wanting to know what the hell was going on; no one had told him I'd been dropped from the client list, and I'm sure Scott was prepared to ship him ghosted Andrew Shaw novels forever, leaving Hamling in the dark and me out of the picture.

There was a flap, and Scott called me and offered to resume representing me. I declined—pride? stupidity? The two, God knows, are not mutually exclusive—and I did finish that one book for Hamling but that was the end of it. We never met.

But I did meet Shorten. He wanted to meet Sheldon Lord and learned that I was in New York. My agent Henry Morrison, unable to figure out a way to prevent it, arranged a meeting at Midwood Tower's midtown office.

I don't remember much about the occasion. It seems to me Midwood had offices on Fifth Avenue in the Forties, but I could be wrong about that. Wherever it was, I went there, and Harry was a bluff and hearty middle-aged fellow. He asked me a few questions, and I did what I could to answer them. He did contrive to bring up the grease pit scene from *Carla* and expressed admiration for my having come up with that one. And he wondered how I managed to get so much sex in without having the books come out dirty. That's not how he worded it, but that seemed to be the gist of it. And I vamped, and said something about writing realistic books about people whose problems and concerns happen to be sexual in nature. I'm not sure what I thought I meant, but I do recall that Harry nodded thoughtfully, and seemed to regard it as a meaningful response.

Harry retired in 1982 and moved to Pompano Beach, Florida. (My Aunt Mim and Uncle Hi lived in Pompano Beach; I wonder if they ever ran into Harry?) He died in 1991, at the age of seventy-six so he must have been around forty-five when we met.

Bob Silverberg, a prolific writer, told me recently that Bill Hamling's still alive and living in Southern California. Maybe I'll drop him a line . . .

CARLA

In the summer of 1958, my buddy Steve Schwerner and I flew from New York to Houston, Texas; hitchhiked to Laredo; disported ourselves across the river in Nuevo Laredo, Mexico; took a bus to Mexico City; did some more disporting; and took another bus to Guadalajara, where a right-wing political party staged a riot while we were trying to get back to our hotel after dinner. A pair of enterprising cops arrested us, threw us in jail overnight, and played bad cop/worse cop with us until we signed over all our traveler's checks, whereupon they put us on a bus back to the border.

So I got home a little earlier than I'd planned.

And one of the things waiting for me at my folks' house in Buffalo was a letter from Henry Morrison, who was then my agent at the Scott Meredith Literary Agency, where I'd been lately employed. "I hope you know what a sex novel is," it began, "and how to write one, because we've got an assignment for you."

Now I'd already written a novel about a young woman's sexual identity crisis in Greenwich Village; Henry had read it and sent it over to Crest Books, then the country's premier publisher of lesbian fiction. They would in time accept it and publish it as *Strange Are the Ways of Love*, but that lay in the future. For now, Henry knew I could start writing a book and get to the end of it, and that was enough to get me this assignment.

The note went on to explain that a fellow named Harry Shorten, who'd created the cartoon "There Oughta Be a Law," had started a publishing house called Midwood Tower. He was looking to develop a line of erotic paperback novels much like those of Beacon Books. And Henry had picked me to write one for him.

Well, OK. I went out and picked up one or two Beacon novels, and if I didn't exactly read them I did look them over to see what they were. They didn't require scrutiny. Because I did know what a sex novel was, and I seemed to know how to write one.

So I went ahead and did just that. The protagonist's name was Carla, and that was my title. *Carla*, by Sheldon Lord.

It never occurred to me, not for a moment, to publish the book under my own name. I wasn't ashamed of it; I didn't think that my writing it was evidence of moral turpitude, but neither did I entertain the notion that it was a contribution to the world of literature. It was a sex novel, for God's sake, and it was to be published by a publisher of sex novels, and what kind of a ninny would put his own name on such a thing?

(Well, Charles Willeford would and did, as I was to find out years later. Some low-rent paperback houses, Beacon among them, published early work of his, and he used his own name.

But Charles was one of a kind, a man who had elevated not giving a rat's ass to the level of an art form. Never mind.)

The name I chose was Sheldon Lord.

Now *Carla* was not the first book I wrote, but it was the first book I sold, and the first to be published. It was not, however, Sheldon Lord's first appearance in print. I'd first used the name when I had two stories slated for the same issue of one of the digest-sized detective story magazines. The editor wanted to use a pen name on one of the stories, and I came up with Sheldon Lord.

(Richard Stark, the name Don Westlake used on all his hard-boiled Parker novels, had a similar origin. Don was sleeping, and a call from his agent awakened him, albeit barely. He had two stories in the same issue of a magazine, and what name would he like on the lesser story? "Richard Stark," Don snarled, and went back to sleep.)

Sheldon Lord. And where did that name come from? Well, I'd known a girl at Antioch College named Marcia Lord, and I really liked her last name. And I liked the name Sheldon, too, though I can't offhand think of anyone who bore it. Sheldon Lord. I used it on that second short story, and I used it on a batch of articles I wrote for a couple of male adventure magazines. (I mean, would you want your own name on "Reinhard Heydrich, Blond Beast of the SS"? Well, neither would I.) There was one similar article I wrote that purported to be an as-told-to piece, and my byline on that one was "by C. O. Jones as told to Sheldon Lord." The editor got the joke and spiked it, changing my evanescent collaborator to C. C. Jones.

Carla, by Sheldon Lord. I sat down in my bedroom on Starin Avenue, at the same maple desk on which I'd written *Strange Are the Ways of Love* a month or two earlier, and I wrote the book and sent it off. Harry Shorten loved it, Henry wrote, but the book wasn't long enough. It needed another chapter. Could I write another chapter to be inserted anywhere in the book?

So I wrote the chapter in which Carla goes on the prowl and winds up with Lou, and we have to wait all the way to the scene's end to realize it would play out a little differently than we'd thought. I sent it in with a note saying that here was a chapter, and it could be inserted anywhere in the book.

The book's set in Buffalo, New York. I was born and grew up in Buffalo and lived there briefly on a couple of occasions after college, but I haven't set much fiction there. Buffalo street names can be found in several of my stories about the criminous criminal lawyer Martin H. Ehrengraf, although their settings remains unspecified. A lost crime novel, one I called *Sinner Man*, had a Buffalo setting; it was sold after many turndowns but doesn't seem ever to have been published, and its setting might as well have been the Bermuda Triangle. The only book in which a Buffalo setting carries any weight is *A Week as Andrea Benstock*, which bore the name Jill Emerson.

Is it significant that my very first published novel takes place in Buffalo? I don't think so. It was a locale of convenience; I was in Buffalo as I wrote the book, so what would be more natural than to set it there? The book itself took the sort of situation James M. Cain and his many imitators used all the time: a triangle with a rich old husband, a hot young wife, and a youthful lower-class lover. Nothing original there, and certainly nothing that screamed Buffalo. I didn't know any people like that, in Buffalo or anywhere else.

By the time I headed off to Antioch College in September, I'd begun to wonder if I was making a mistake. What did I need with college?

I'd just had a year off. When I landed an editorial job at the Scott Meredith Literary Agency the previous summer, I'd realized there was more to learn there than on campus, and I dropped out. By the following spring I'd been working long enough and was ready to go back to school.

But now I'd not only published a slew of short stories and articles, but I'd actually written two novels and sold one of them, and the guy who'd bought *Carla* was hungry for more. He wanted another book and seemed likely to want more after that.

(What sold Harry Shorten, it turned out, was the scene in the grease pit, which gives *down and dirty* a whole other meaning. When I actually met Shorten, a couple of books later, he kept talking about the grease pit scene in *Carla*. Now I don't think I'd ever *seen* a grease pit. I just sort of knew that they had them in service stations, so the grease would have someplace to go. You know what they tell you about writing what you know? Well, the hell with that.)

All I wanted, all I'd ever wanted, was to be a writer. Not a journalist—I knew I didn't want to have to ask people questions they didn't want to answer. I wanted to make things up. I wanted to write novels, and get paid for them, and have people—women, in particular—read them and admire me.

Well, I wasn't sure the best way to win female admiration was by writing about Carla and the grease pit. Still, as I braced myself for a class at Antioch College on the eighteenth century English novel, I couldn't help but wonder: What the hell was I doing there?

COMMUNITY OF WOMEN

Ah yes, *Community of Women*. Both the title and the book's premise originated with someone at Beacon Books. I don't know his name, but I would give odds he was a fellow who put on a jacket and tie every morning and drove to the train station. And as his commuter train pulled away from the platform, bound for Grand Central, he found himself looking out the window and thinking about all the women who were left behind while their husbands went off to earn a living in the concrete canyons of Manhattan. *All those women*, he thought. *Women in the bloom of youth, women beginning to ripen into their full sexual maturity. Women, all of them, with no men around, and here I am stuck on this fucking train . . .*

How often did he have this thought? Five days a week, you figure? And how many weeks before he picked up the phone and called a literary agent with whom he'd done some business. "I've got an idea for a book," he said. "Oh, I dunno. It just sort of came to me. Maybe that new guy could do it. What's his name, Sheldon Lord? Maybe he could do it."

Indeed.

I was away from my desk when my agent, Henry Morrison, relayed the call from the horny commuter at Beacon. My desk was in my apartment in Manhattan, and my wife and daughter and I were in Buffalo, New York, visiting family. We were staying in the house I grew up in, on Starin Avenue, and I know that because I remember writing *Community of Women* on the card table in the sun room, which was what we called the front parlor.

"They have this idea for a book," Henry told me, and recounted the title and premise. "But here's the thing, they need it Right Away."

Now this was not the first time I'd been told that somebody needed something Right Away. And here's the weird thing— I always believed it, and I always acted accordingly. This may

stem from my training, during the not-quite-a-year I spent as
an editor at the Scott Meredith Literary Agency. Every once in
a while some magazine editor would call up, having suddenly
discovered that he had a hole in an issue that was about to go to
press. Someone who'd promised to deliver something had failed,
or somebody pulled an ad, or—well, it didn't matter. Some editorial content was required, and did Scott have a writer handy
who could deliver the thing soon? Say yesterday, for instance?

It was those of us in the office—editors by day, writers by
night—to whom these prizes would be offered. One learned the
only proper answer to the question, "can you do this?" was, "yes,
of course." Could you write a medical confession story? A male
adventure article? Yes, of course you could. And could you bring
it in tomorrow morning? You bet.

Because, if it was that urgent, it was also a sure sale. You still
made sure you turned in something professional and as good as
you could make it in the time available, because you wanted them
to turn to you again. But it was more important that it be done
than it be done superbly, and that was clear to all concerned.

But there was a difference between a magazine editor with a
hole in his issue and a book editor with a hole in his head, and I
never learned to make the distinction. Beacon couldn't possibly
need *Community of Women* right away. But that's what I was
told, and I acted accordingly.

I think the first time this had happened was in the summer
of 1960. I had been married in March and was living at 110
West Sixty-ninth Street. A mystery writer named William Ard
had died at the age of 37, leaving a young widow and an incom-
plete manuscript. While I couldn't be expected to do anything
about the former, I'd been chosen to finish the book, which was
under contract to Monarch Books.

And they needed it Right Away!

Oh, like hell they did. What urgency could such a project possibly have. Did they have a cover? A firm publication date? No, of course not. But these were questions that never occurred to me. I rose to the occasion, sort of, by taking a room down the street from our apartment, at a hotel on the corner of Broadway and Sixty-ninth. (There were two hotels at that intersection, the Sherman Square and the Spencer Arms, and I took a room at one of them. The one on the southeast corner, whichever it was.) Ard was a pro, with a string of mysteries and westerns, and he probably would have made the book work; on the other hand, it may have taken some of the sting out of dying to know that he wouldn't have to finish it. He left behind a couple of chapters and an outline, and I'm sure he'd have departed from the outline and come up with something that made a little more sense. I probably departed from the outline myself, it was impossible not to, but I didn't agonize over it because the folks at Monarch needed this Right Away.

So I went to my rented room each morning, and worked all day, and went home to have dinner with my wife, and went back for a few more hours of writing. I don't know how long it took me to deliver the book, but it had to be less than a week. If the people at Monarch hated it, they kept it to themselves. It was published: *Babe in the Woods, a Lou Largo Novel by William Ard.* John Jakes, who went on to make a very big name for himself as a writer of historical fiction, ghosted three more Lou Largo novels, but he got to plot them himself; I'm sure they were a lot better than mine.

I wonder if they told him they needed the books Right Away.

Well, if Beacon needed *Community of Women* right away, that's how they would get it. And to tell you the truth, I welcomed the pressure. It gave me something to do while we were in Buffalo.

I wrote the book over a weekend. Three, four days. Something like that. It seems to me it went reasonably well, but I can't say I remember much of the plot or characters. I might recognize elements if I were to read the book, but toward what end? It's by not reading my early work that I'm able to agree to make it available once again.

I do remember one character. He's a writer, and his name is Lincoln Barclay, and he's the rare man to be found home during the daytime in this suburban wonderland. Which of course gives him opportunities for adventure.

Oh, really? A writer, you say, getting all that Westchester County action? A writer with the initials LB?

Hey, the editor on the train had his fantasies. Why shouldn't I have mine?

GIGOLO JOHNNY WELLS

My first book for Bill Hamling's Nightstand Books, and Andrew Shaw's first appearance in print, was *Campus Tramp*. I wrote it in the summer of 1959 in my furnished room at the Hotel Rio, on West Forty-seventh Street between Sixth and Seventh Avenues. That was a fascinating block at the time, before the southward expansion of Rockefeller Center performed a sort of corporate urban renewal. In another book (also by Andrew Shaw, and published by Nightstand) I listed the restaurants and other places of business on that one block. One of the Broadway columnists designated that particular block *Dream Street*, and while that sobriquet may have been fastened on other parts of Times Square, I always figured the guy had it right.

There was, God knows, nothing fancy about the Rio, but it was a decent place, family owned and operated. A lot of Greek seamen stayed there when they made port in New York as well as the usual mix of up-and-comers and down-and-outers, in and out of the arts, that you'd get in a low-rent residential hotel. I only lived there for a month or two that summer, but two years later, when I was living uptown on Central Park West, I used a room at the Rio as an office.

Campus Tramp may have been Andrew Shaw's first book, but not mine. A little more than a year earlier I'd written a lesbian novel that Crest Books would publish as *Strange Are the Ways of Love*. Then I wrote *Carla* for Harry Shorten's new operation, Midwood Tower, and returned to Antioch College for what would be my final year of college, though I didn't know it at the time. There was a three month stretch when I edited the college newspaper, and I gave that my full attention, but otherwise what I mostly did was drink and smoke dope and fool around with women.

And write. Harry Shorten was crazy about *Carla* and wanted more, so instead of reading *Humphry Clinker* and *Roderick Random* and *Joseph Andrews*, I was writing *A Strange Kind of Love* and *69 Barrow Street* and *Born to Be Bad*. I'd gone off to college in the first place so that I could become a writer, and I was damned if I was going to let my education get in the way of my work.

When the school year ended I returned to New York and took a room at the Rio, and even as I was delivering the next Midwood book to my agent, he had an assignment for me. A new publisher, Nightstand Books, wanted a book and they'd pay seven hundred fifty dollars, which was a cut above the six hundred dollars I was getting from Shorten. Thus *Campus Tramp*.

And the book went over fine with Hamling, who let me know via my agent that he could use a book a month from Andrew Shaw.

A book a month. Maybe Harry Shorten would have taken a book of month from me, were I to write them that frequently, but Bill Hamling virtually insisted on it. Did it ever occur to me that I might have trouble turning out work at that rate? I honestly don't think it ever did. The books had to be two hundred pages long, and it wasn't that hard to produce twenty pages a day, and to do that five or six days a week. So do the math—two weeks to fulfill my obligation to Nightstand and two weeks to write the books I cared about—which probably meant crime fiction of one sort or another.

Piece of cake.

Let's not forget there was ample frosting on that piece of cake, and it was sweet frosting indeed. You didn't get rich writing books at seven hundred fifty dollars a pop, each of which netted you six hundred seventy-five dollars after your agent's commission. (My agent at the time got more than his ten percent, we learned many years later. He also got a hefty packaging fee from Hamling.) You didn't get rich but you didn't go hungry, either, and this was at a time when big corporations were hiring college graduates for five thousand dollars a year. But corporations wouldn't have hired me—I wasn't a college graduate—and six hundred seventy-five dollars a month was a whole lot better than what they paid you to bag groceries.

And it left me half the month to write something else! It would be nice to report that I devoted that second half of the month to serious fiction, or at least to fiction that I was serious about, but most of the time I spent it writing the odd book for Harry Shorten, or handling some assignment my agent came up with. Psychosexual case histories under a medical pen name. A quickie ghostwriting job for the publisher of *Confidential* magazine, who wanted me to cut and paste a bushel full of old magazine pieces into a book. An adventure novel for Monarch Books—*Fidel Castro Assassinated!*

Nothing to make John Steinbeck eat his heart out.

No matter. It wasn't long before Hamling raised his boys to one thousand dollars a book. That was too good to turn down, and it all served another important function as well. It kept me from having to figure out what I really wanted to write.

And what has any of this to do with *Gigolo Johnny Wells*?

Well, I'm not sure. But thinking about the book has brought those Nightstand days into focus for me. It's hard to see the picture when you're standing inside the frame, and it's easier to have some perspective on the time now that half a century (half a century!) has slipped by.

I've often said that I don't regret the books I wrote early on, or the time I spent writing them. I've always regarded those days as a paid apprenticeship. You learn how to write by writing, and that's what I did and how I did it.

At the same time, it seems to me that I stayed too long at the fair. Under the aegis of the Scott Meredith Literary Agency, where they always took the cash and let the credit go, I accepted the assignments and went for the sure money.

The Nightstand books became part of my monthly routine, and in time the writing of them became itself routine. Each book was the work of ten writing days—or, if I buckled down and wrote forty pages a day instead of twenty, just five days work. They were spun, I'm sure, out of some unconscious synthesis of experience and imagination. I developed no end of tricks to fill pages rapidly, stacking up one-sentence paragraphs, ending chapters at the top rather than the bottom of a typed page, and letting conversations go on as long as the characters felt like nattering away at each other.

My second daughter was born in May of 1963, and I had the obstetrician's bill to pay. That month I did an extra book for Nightstand. I wrote eighty-five pages the first day, eighty the second, and finished the book early in the afternoon of the third day. I have no idea which book it was; two days later, the names of the characters and every detail of the plot had vanished from my memory. I don't think the book ever imprinted there in the first place. I just channeled it onto the page, put it in the mail, and that was the end of it.

Still, some of the books were better than others. Once in a while a character or situation resonated sufficiently with me that I did better work and produced a better book. I didn't think anyone would notice, and barely noticed myself. But *Gigolo Johnny Wells* (which was published as *Lover*) was a cut above the rest, and I knew it at the time. I wasn't tempted to try it somewhere else because it was still quite clearly a Nightstand book, but I sent it off feeling good about it, and whoever read it at Nightstand felt the same way. (Harlan Ellison, I believe. Harlan was Hamling's anonymous editor for a stretch, before Algis Budrys took over. *Gigolo Johnny Wells* was published in 1961, so it would have been written that year or the year before, which would probably put it in Harlan's time.)

The editor read it, and liked it. And how did he reward me for my superior performance?

He requested a sequel.

You know, the last thing I wanted to do was write a second book about Johnny Wells. I'd already told the world all I had to say about him, and then some. But I had to write something, and this is what they wanted me to write, so I did it.

And I wish I could figure out what became of it. All I remember about it is that Johnny went downhill. His life turned on him and I think either drink or drugs got hold of him; it wasn't a pretty picture. At the end of the book, I made damn certain I'd never be asked to write further about the poor son of a bitch. By the time I typed *The End*, it had all ended forever for Gigolo Johnny. He no longer had a pulse, and I was spared turning him into a series character.

But I can't find the book. I wrote it, and Hamling published it, but I've no idea what he might have called it or where I might find a copy. If you run across it, let me know, will you? I won't claim you'll be performing a great service to American letters, but you'll be doing me a favor.

About the name.

As the new title alone would suggest, the hero's name is Johnny Wells. A couple of years after I wrote this book I began using the pseudonym John Warren Wells on psycho-sexual nonfiction books, mainly collections of fabricated case histories.

There was no conscious connection between the character and the pen name. Three or four years separated the death of one and the emergence of the other, and I doubt I could have told you the character's surname by the time I selected the pen name.

During those years, I was writing eighteen or twenty books a year—a dozen for Nightstand, plus a batch for other houses. Each of those books had a slew of characters and all of those characters had names, and I'm sure I repeated names from time to time. I must have chosen both names, Johnny Wells and John

Warren Wells, the way I picked most character names. I liked the way they sounded.

A STRANGE KIND OF LOVE

In the summer of 1958 I came home from an aborted Mexican holiday. Waiting for me, in my parents' house in Buffalo, New York, was a letter from my agent. It contained an assignment and led to my writing an erotic novel that took a James M. Cain situation, left out the menace and violence (along with the gritty realism and literary merit), and included a memorable scene in which the titular heroine—and I use the adjective advisedly—copulated with a gas pump jockey in the grease pit of his service station.

Eat your heart out, Jimmy Cain.

I called the book *Carla* and sent it to my agent, who sent it to Harry Shorten at Midwood Tower. Harry liked it, and flat-out *loved* the grease pit scene. He published it and asked for more.

But by then I was back at school.

I'd spent two years at Antioch College, during which I'd neither covered myself with glory nor gotten myself expelled. In the summer after my second year I got a job at the Scott Meredith Literary Agency, where I read amateur work and told the fee-paying writers what was wrong with it. (Every report I wrote, I should say, was a work of fiction, because my job was to tell them they were fine writers—they were not— and that it was a failure of plot that kept their story from working. It wasn't the plot, it was that they were talentless saps who couldn't write their name in the dirt with a stick. But if I told them that they wouldn't send in more stories, with more fees, and Scott never met a dollar he could bring himself to turn down.)

Irrespective of what it did for such moral character as I possessed, the job was the best possible training ground for a writer. You learn more reading bad work than good work, because it's so much easier to see what's wrong with something than what's right with it. Long story short, I knew the first week that this was too good a job to leave after two months. I dropped out of college and stayed in New York for the better part of the year. I left in May, and by autumn I was back at school, wondering what I was doing there.

Then I got a letter and learned that Harry Shorten would love for me to do another book for him. Ah, that was the answer. I now knew what I was doing in Yellow Springs, Ohio. I was writing a second book for Harry Shorten.

A defining component of the program at Antioch College is its co-op program; students spend half the year on campus and the other half in jobs designed to provide life and vocational experience. One of my own co-op jobs, for example, had been in the mail room at Pines Publications. That job had been obtained through the school's co-op department, while I'd found the one at Scott Meredith on my own.

Now I was back at school after a year away. I was scheduled to spend January through March as the full-time editor of *The Record*, Antioch's college paper; that would be my co-op job for that period. Prior to that I'd be a full-time student for three months, taking a couple of English courses and something called Workshop in Small-Group Functioning, which had looked interesting, but wasn't. In addition to my courses, I'd be assisting *Record* editor Bob Zevin, and thus learning what I had to know to take over in January.

I did put in a lot of time at the *Record*. And it was in the *Record* office, on the second floor of the Student Union, that I wrote *A Strange Kind of Love*.

I don't know how long it took, or how often I worked on it. I remember sitting alone in the *Record* office, after everyone else had gone home. Most of the work at the paper seemed to get done at night, so it was generally quite late when I put in my time at the typewriter, telling the story of a broken-down writer who gets himself together, all for the love of a good woman, and then returns almost gratefully to the gutter when his romance lands in the crapper.

Now and then a fee-paying writer had submitted a story to Scott Meredith with a writer or some other artist as a lead character, and that always gave me an opening to reject it. The average reader, I knew enough to say, has trouble identifying with artistic types or relating to their problems. (Was that ever true? Maybe, but it seems way off the mark nowadays. If, as Napoleon had it, every French soldier carries in his knapsack the baton of a Marshal of France, so does virtually every reader of novels imagine himself as an author, and a successful one at that.)

Did it occur to me, in the stillness of an Ohio night, that I was cheerfully violating the rules I'd laid down for others? I doubt I ever gave it a thought, and why should I? At Midwood, and the following year at Nightstand Books, a handful of writers were essentially inventing a new kind of book, furnishing product to fill a demand the marketplace hadn't known existed.

And the demand was unmistakably present. Midwood and Nightstand were wildly successful from the day their first titles hit the stands. We who wrote the books did so for a flat rate so we didn't get royalties, but if we had we'd have made a lot of money. Readers liked these books, and apparently couldn't get enough of them.

I didn't know this then, but I knew Harry Shorten wasn't going to mind if my lead character was a writer. Just so there was a sex scene in every chapter, restrained enough to keep him out of jail, but sufficiently stimulating so that the reader would endeavor to turn the pages with one hand. So to speak.

And did I have an actual writer in mind?

No, of course not. If my lead character was anybody—and I'm by no means sure that he was—then he was my own self, projected into a possible future. I'd read *Skid Row U.S.A.*, by Sara Harris, and found the notion of a descent to the Bowery a reasonably romantic fantasy. I could as readily envision myself ending up in a flophouse sucking on a bottle of muscatel as reading leather-bound books by the fireside in the library of my Westport estate.

In the fullness of time, I came closer to the former than the latter. But I didn't know that then. All I knew was that I had a book to finish, and that I'd better see how much of it I could get done before the sun came up and it was too late to work.

Other Pseudonymous Novels

PASSPORT TO PERIL

In 1966 I was living at 16 Stratford Place in New Brunswick, New Jersey. I'd spent a year in Wisconsin as an editor in the coin supply division of Western Printing, and just when it looked as though I might have a future in the corporate world, I realized it was the last thing I wanted. I'd been writing books all along, and I moved east and resumed writing full-time.

My agent, Henry Morrison, came to me with an assignment. Lancer Books, for whom I'd written a few books during Larry T. Shaw's editorship, wanted to publish a romantic espionage thriller in the tradition of Helen MacInnes. I hadn't read anything by Ms. MacInnes, though I knew the byline; her books were published in hardcover and frequently wound up on bestseller lists. Mine would be published as a paperback original, and bestseller status would be not even a fleeting dream.

I don't know if I actually read any of the books which were to be my model. I probably skimmed a couple. I knew what was required—a clean, sweet, likable American girl as the heroine;

a reasonably exotic foreign locale; and a couple of people who were not what they appeared to be, including an evident villain who would become the unlikely hero and love interest and a dashingly attractive good guy who would turn out to be an absolute rotter.

I could do that.

I knew just where to set it. Ireland. Where else?

I'd actually been to Ireland, which gave it a leg up on the rest of the world. In the fall of 1964, a few months after a move to Racine, Wisconsin, my wife and I flew to Limerick and spent the better part of two weeks driving around Ireland. We spent a day in Edinburgh, Scotland and a few days in England, but Ireland got the bulk of our business.

Aside from brief forays into Canada and Mexico, this was my first time out of the States, and if it felt like an adventure, it felt even more like a homecoming. It's clear to me that I spent at least one past life in Ireland. Among my earliest memories are of listening to Irish songs on the radio. (There was a girl who sang "Too-ra-loo-ra-loo-ral, That's an Irish Lullaby" on a local amateur show, and I'm pleased to report that she was the winner three weeks running.) I had a set of *The Book of Knowledge*, and from it I learned all the words to "The Wearin' o' the Green."

When I had begun selling short fiction and was casting about for a book to write, I decided a novel of the Irish rebellion and civil war might be a good choice. But what did I know about it? I amassed an extensive library of English and Irish history and read a surprising amount of it. Around the time that my interest in numismatics (currency) was steering me toward the job in Wisconsin, I began collecting Irish coins, tokens, and medals.

No question, then. I'd set the book in Ireland.

Ever since the trip, I'd been picking up records of Irish

folk music. The Clancy Brothers, of course, but also a slew of Folkways albums on which various singers, some more gifted than others, collected songs of the 1798 Rising and other blighted periods in the land's sad history. As G. K. Chesterton wrote:

> For the great Gaels of Ireland
> Are the men that God made mad,
> For all their wars are merry,
> And all their songs are sad.

Well, why not make my heroine a folksinger? Why not send her to Ireland to collect songs? There, of course, she could meet the wolf in sheep's clothing and the sheep in wolf's clothing, and things could look decidedly dark for a while, but eventually the sun would burst through. I mean, it would have to, sooner or later. As far as we could make out, it was always either raining or about to rain in Ireland, but maybe I could cheat and have a little sunshine toward the end.

I went to New York to write the book. Don Westlake had sublet a studio apartment on West Twenty-fourth Street in Chelsea; he'd lived there briefly during a marital rough spot, and kept it as a sometimes office until the lease was up. I moved in and brought home *Passport to Peril* ten days later. I don't know if the title was mine, though I rather think it was. I know the pen name was mine, and I know that forty-five years later nobody else on earth knew it.

Henry knew back then, but I'm sure he's long since forgotten. My first wife would have known, but I don't think she ever read the book, and I would be surprised if she recalls anything about it. Irwin Stein at Lancer would have known but would have had no reason to remember. Among the book-collecting fraternity, no one had a clue. This book, and *Fidel Castro Assassinated*, are the two works of mine that somehow escaped detection. The latter, written under the name Lee Duncan, was recently reprinted as *Killing Castro* by Hard Case Crime. *Passport to Peril* now makes its first post-Lancer appearance as an ebook, and I can only hope you've enjoyed it.

I read it myself recently to ready it for publication, and I was surprised to find that I liked it. Remember what William Butler Yeats wrote?

> Romantic Ireland's dead and gone,
> It's with O'Leary in the grave.

True, too, of the Ireland of the 1960s. It was a curious pleasure to revisit the time and place, if in my own work.

STRANGE ARE THE WAYS OF LOVE

While I was a student at Antioch College, someone posted a cartoon on the English department bulletin board. It showed a school official telling a very small boy, "But it's not enough to be a genius, Arnold. You have to be a genius *at* something."

Some years earlier, in Miss May Jepson's third-year English class at Bennett High School in Buffalo, New York, I'd realized that I wanted to be a writer. Although I'd always been a reader, I'd lately become a reader of modern American fiction—books for grown-ups, if you will, since the term *adult fiction* has come to mean something manifestly different and not for grown-ups at all.

I was reading James T. Farrell and John Steinbeck and

Thomas Wolfe, and I was writing poems and brief sketches, and I had the insight that writing for a living was at once something I would enjoy and something I might be able to do. From then on I never seriously considered doing anything else.

I won the office of Senior Class Poet. (I'd submitted two entries, one in Imagist-style free verse, the other in orotund iambic pentameter. Entries were anonymous, but Miss Jepson later confided that she'd recognized both as my work. They placed first and second, with orotundity carrying the day.) I graduated high school and went off to Antioch, where I wrote more poetry and some faltering short stories. The summer after my second year I spent a couple of weeks on Cape Cod, Massachusetts, living in an honest-to-God garret and writing a story every day. One of them became my first sale.

From the Cape I went to New York, where I got a job at a literary agency telling wannabes what was wrong with their stories, and why they should try again and pay another reading fee. I spent evenings writing and sold a batch of stories and fielded assignments that came my way, articles for male-interest magazines ("Reinhard Heydrich, Blond Beast of the SS!"), and medical confession mags ("My name is Brad Haviland. I'm forty-two years old, and I'm the best bowel surgeon in the state.")

But what I really wanted to do was write a novel.

Now on the face of it I didn't have the same problem as Arnold, the little boy in the cartoon. If it wasn't enough to be a writer, if you actually had to write something, well, I was doing that—and selling most of what I wrote, albeit to low-paying markets. But if I wanted to be a novelist I had to write a novel, and I didn't have a novel to write.

Some writers seem to be born with particular stories to

tell. Whether it's their own life or their fantasy world that provides them with source material, they know what they want to write almost before they know they want to write anything.

Not so with me. What I knew was I wanted to be a writer, and I'd have written just about anything toward that end. The first thing I sold was a crime story, published by *Manhunt* magazine, and once they bought it I found myself coming up with other stories in that vein. But I'd tried other kinds of stories, too, and if one of them had sold I'd have found myself veering off in another direction altogether.

A senior editor at the Scott Meredith Literary Agency suggested I try a nurse novel. A publisher named Thomas Bouregy had an imprint called Avalon Books, with a line of hardcover nurse novels that were a staple of rental library fiction. The books ran around forty-five thousand words, and while they weren't terribly lucrative—I think the writers got something like four hundred dollars a book—it was a fairly easy place to break in. And I sensed that I'd learn something by writing forty-five thousand words of continuous narrative. My stories tended to be short, and I was inclined to wrap things up in two thousand words even though the market preferred them two or three times that long.

I read a couple of nurse novels, but I couldn't begin to think of how I could write one. Instead I tried a crime novel, a first-person effort that owed a lot to Fredric Brown's first novel, *The Fabulous Clipjoint*. It was hopeless, not least because I couldn't think of anything for my characters to do. I gave up forty or fifty pages into it, and not a moment too soon.

Then one night I went bar-hopping in the Village, and for no particular reason I got very drunk that night. I was living at the Hotel Alexandria, at Broadway and 103rd, and somebody poured me into a cab and sent me home. I woke up the next morning with an absolutely murderous hangover.

And it was an unusual hangover at that, because I awoke full of creative energy, awoke with an idea for a novel. It was just there. I don't know where it came from, but there it was, and I wasn't inclined to let it get away.

Now I didn't have to go into the office, because I'd received a sort of promotion; I now brought home a sackful of fee manuscripts read them on my own time, wrote the requisite reports, and turned up once a week to hand in my work and replenish my supply.

So I didn't have to go anywhere while my hangover burned so brightly, nor did I have to do anything.

I sat down and wrote a two-page chapter-by-chapter outline of a novel. I had the whole thing there—the setting, the plot, the characters. All I had to do was write it, and I somehow knew that wouldn't be a problem.

Nor was it. I'd dropped out of Antioch for a year to get what I could out of the job at Scott Meredith. After the better part of a year I figured it was time to drop back in again before the draft got me. I'd start in the fall, after spending the summer in Mexico with my friend Steve Schwerner. So sometime in May I wrapped things up at Scott Meredith, checked out of the Alexandria, and took the train back home to Buffalo to spend some time with my folks before Steve and I headed south.

While I was home, I wrote *Strange Are the Ways of Love.* The idea may have come in a burst of post-alcoholic energy, but I'd already thought of writing a lesbian novel. I read a great deal of lesbian fiction and nonfiction, some by Marijane Meaker under one name or another. I'm sure I read them in part out of prurient interest, but that's why I initially read John O'Hara, James T. Farrell, and no end of fine writers. And it was more than the hope of titillation that brought me back to the lesbian novels. Somehow or other I identified with the characters. And, somehow or other, I identified with the authors; I knew I could write this sort of book.

Well, I was right about that. I sat down at my desk in my bedroom on Starin Avenue, outline at hand, and each day I wrote a chapter. In two weeks I was done. I called the book *Shadows*— that's the name of the bar where much of the story's action takes place, loosely modeled on a Macdougal Street establishment called Swing Rendezvous. I wrapped up the manuscript and sent it off to Henry Morrison at Scott Meredith. Steve showed up in Buffalo, and the two of us went to Mexico.

Henry read the manuscript and submitted it to the premier market for lesbian novels, the Crest Books imprint at Fawcett Publications. In the fall I was back at Antioch, writing books for Harry Shorten at Midwood Tower, editing the college newspaper, and neglecting my schoolwork, when Henry wrote to tell me that Crest wanted to publish the book. And they were going to pay me two thousand dollars, which was more than three times what I was getting from Midwood.

I went to New York over Christmas break, and met with the folks at Crest. I remember I met with Bill Lengel and Leona Nevler and with the young woman who would be my editor, and whose name I recall as Nancy Holley. She was a tall blonde, a fairly recent graduate of one of the Seven Sisters colleges, and they'd given her my book to practice on.

Back at Antioch, I worked on the revisions. I don't think they could have amounted to much, but whatever she asked me to do, I went and did. I was new enough at this to think that's what you had to do. Years later I would read John O'Hara's pronunciamento that, once he'd finished a story, the only way he improved it was by telling an editor to go to hell. Who knew you could do that?

There was at least one time when I should have told Nancy Holley to go to hell, and that was when she told me to cut a chapter. As you'll have noted, each subordinate character has a chapter from his or her point of view, and the one who doesn't—but did—is Peggy, the girl whom Jan replaces in Laura's affections. Peggy's chapter began "Her name was Peggy Corcoran and she was drunk." And indeed she was, and she managed to get cornered by a pack of street toughs, who beat her up and raped her. It was a perfectly good chapter, and it provided a glimpse of some of the dangers inherent in the life, and the only reason it's not in the book is that Nancy Holley thought it should come out.

Nancy wherever you are, go to hell, will you?

The title, I was informed, would be *Strange Are the Ways of Love.*

OK, I said.

And I would need a female pen name. It seems to me I came up with one, although I can't recall it, but someone at Crest decided to improve on it. The name they gave me was Leslie Evans. That way, see, the name was gender-ambiguous. Leslie could be a man or a woman. Like, whatever.

OK, I said.

Then they changed the spelling. They picked the name for its ambiguity and then spelled it Lesley, so it could only be a woman's name.

OK, I said.

Strange Are the Ways of Love should have launched me as a

lesbian novelist. But it took a while. I kept going for the sure money, writing soft-core erotica for Midwood and Nightstand Books. I never managed to come up with an idea for Lesley Evans's second book. When I did, Lesley Evans was long forgotten, and the book—*Warm and Willing*—was a first book for Jill Emerson.

Many years later I was on Terry Gross's NPR show, *Fresh Air*, to talk about my lesbian body of work. During one off-mike moment, Terry said, "But Larry, you're not a lesbian."

"Terry," I said, "that's technically true. But it's only an accident of birth."

STRANGE EMBRACE

I don't seem to remember writing *Strange Embrace*.

Oh, I know it's mine. I can tell by flipping through it that I did indeed write it, and in fact I remember having written it. But I have no recollection of being at work on the book, or where I was when I wrote it. I'm pretty sure I know what I was paid for writing it—$1,000, as I recall, which would come to $900 for me and $100 for Scott Meredith, who was representing me at the time. I know there were never any royalties (or if they were, they were all for Scott Meredith.) I've learned through the miracle of Google Books that an Australian edition was published, with the title changed to *Act One: Murder!* and Ben Christopher's name on the cover, and that never brought me a dime, or the Aussie equivalent thereof.

I'm not complaining, mind you. Just letting you know what I remember, and what I don't.

Strange Embrace started life as an assignment, which came to me from Beacon Books via Scott Meredith. What they wanted was a mystery novel of 50,000 words or so based on a TV series called *Johnny Midnight*. Edmund O'Brien played Johnny, a theatrical producer with a wise-cracking Japanese houseboy. The series ran for 39 episodes in 1959–60, which is to say it ran for a year. Back then you ran new stories for nine months and then gave way to a summer replacement. Nowadays a full season is what, 26 episodes? 22?

Well, it turns out that 39 episodes of *Johnny Midnight* was more than enough. Edmund O'Brien's girth may have had something to do with this. He'd put on a substantial amount of weight since he starred in the noir film classic, *D.O.A.*, and the producers of the TV show tried to save things by putting the poor sonofabitch on a crash vegetarian diet. He may have lost a pound or two, but he didn't pick up many viewers, and the network waved bye-bye after a single season.

Now this was not the first TV show shot out from under me. That distinction belongs to *Markham,* which starred Ray Milland, and which also quit the airways after a single season. And, *mirabile dictu*, both of these TV wonders emanated from the same studio. (Revue, back then, later Universal Studios.)

What exactly did they want me to do?

Beacon Books wanted me to write a tie-in novel. I'd be making use of the characters from the TV series and fashioning an original plot for them. There were a lot of TV tie-in novels back then, and I guess they sold well enough, if the shows on which they were based were themselves popular. If not, not; if nobody would watch the show for free, why would anyone shell out 35¢ to read a printed version thereof?

So that was the assignment, and I said okay. Why not? I'd already done this sort of thing once by then.

In fact I'd done it twice. It was Belmont Books that commissioned *Markham,* and I sat down and wrote it, and it turned out rather well. At least I thought so, and I showed it to Don Westlake, and he thought so, too. and Henry Morrison (who represented me at Scott Meredith) read it and agreed with both of us, and sent it over to Knox Burger at Gold Medal, who bought it and paid me $2,500 for it. I changed Roy Markham's name to Ed London and called the book *Coward's Kiss,* and Gold Medal changed the title to *Death Pulls a Doublecross,* and it came out in due course as the second book published under my own name. (It's since been republished a few times, and it's *Coward's Kiss* once again. If you can just outlast the bastards, sooner or later you get to set things right.)

Then I had to fulfill my obligation to Belmont, and I wrote a book I called *Markham,* and they kept the title and added a subtitle: *The Case of the Pornographic Photos.* Isn't that catchy? It sounds like Nancy Drew gone wrong. It's now available as an Open Road ebook with the title I gave it when a paperback publisher reprinted it some years ago: *You Could Call It Murder.* It has my name on it, but then it always did.

Strange Embrace.

I was living in New York when I wrote it, but whether it was just before or just after we moved from 110 West Sixty-ninth Street to 444 Central Park West I couldn't tell you.

I do know this much: By the time I delivered the book, which wouldn't have been more than three weeks after I started work on it, *Johnny Midnight* was history. The same fate fell upon *Markham,* but Belmont went ahead and published it all the same, fulfilling their agreement with Revue, and perhaps figuring that the Ray Milland connection wouldn't hurt the book's chances, even if the series was toast. Maybe there was no way to get out of their contract with Revue. Who knows? The series was dead, but the book went to the printer all the same.

It was a different story at Beacon. They had to buy the book, they were fine with the book, but why pay money to a TV studio to tie in with a piece-of-shit series that nobody watched in the first place? So one of their editors went to work, changing Johnny's last name from Midnight to Lane. (Hey, why not? It could have been worse. "There but for the grace of God goes Johnny Daybreak.")

They hung their own title on it. I'd called it *Johnny Midnight,* imaginatively enough, and they picked *Strange Embrace,* which gave me a titular hat trick—three novels under three different names, each with the word *strange* in it. (*Strange Are the Ways of Love,* by Lesley Evans; *A Strange Kind of Love,* by Sheldon Lord; and, duh, *Strange Embrace,* by Ben Christopher.) Each title was the publisher's contribution. Nobody asked me.

Neat, huh? I'd have to call it weird. Even eerie. Or—what's the word Im looking for?

Oh, right. *Strange.*

About the pen name.

Why did I use one? If my first tie-in novel, *Markham,* was respectable enough to have my own name on it, why slap a pen name on *Johnny Midnight?*

I don't remember what I was thinking at the time, but my guess is that it had something to do with the publisher. Beacon was a pretty cheesy house, a second-rate publisher of soft-core erotica, and who would put his own name on a Beacon book? (Well, Charles Willeford would and did, but then it's hard to find a rule to which Charles wasn't an exception. Fine man, brilliant writer, and sui generis as all get out.)

But why Ben Christopher?

Right around this time, my great good friend Don Westlake also wrote a TV tie-in, and used the name Ben Christopher on it. It was, he said, his name for tie-ins. Well, how would it be if I used it for one of mine? He said it would be fine, because he figured he was done with it, and done with tie-ins.

So just now I tried to find out what tie-in novel Don did, and it turned out he didn't—not a book, that is. He seems to have used the name one time only, on a story that appeared in *77 Sunset Strip Magazine.* It was very likely the lead story, unquestionably a tie in, and probably novella length. But it wasn't a book. I seem to be the only person to have used the name Ben Christopher on a book.

Strange, innit?

HELLCATS AND HONEY GIRLS TRILOGY, WITH DONALD E. WESTLAKE

In August of 1957 I answered a blind ad, took a test, and landed a job as an assistant editor at the Scott Meredith Literary Agency, where I spent my days reading amateur work and writing encouraging rejections. (Encouraging because we wanted the authors to submit more material, accompanied by more reading fees; rejections because the stuff was, by and large, terrible.) It was a great learning experience for a writer-in-training and by the time I left there the following May, I had sold a slew of short stories and articles. The first thing I did when I got home to Buffalo, New York, was write a novel, and I wrote a batch more in the months that followed. I was by then back at Antioch College in Yellow Springs, Ohio, and was supposed to be writing papers for my professors. Instead I was writing soft-core sex novels for Harry Shorten of Midwood Tower.

Around this time, Don Westlake answered the same ad, took the same test, and landed the same job. And he, too, began writing for Harry Shorten at Midwood; I first became aware of him when I read his first Midwood title, *All My Lovers*, by one Alan Marshall. I remember a scene where the brothers of a slum girl, who's been led astray by a young executive type, go to the rotter's luxurious apartment and beat the crap out of him. Then they leave and the scene closes with these lines: "They did not take anything. They were not thieves."

I thought that was pretty damn good and wondered who'd written it.

A few months later Don got his first look at me, although it might have been through a one-way mirror for all I saw of him. I was in New York City on Christmas break and had gone to the Scott Meredith office, where I was now a client—though not the sort whose picture they put on the wall for all to see. There was a sliding window in the antechamber where they hadn't put my picture, and my agent Henry Morrison and I talked through a book project. And Don was in the bullpen office on the other side of that window and saw me, although I did not see him.

And this was the conversation he overheard:

"That last book I delivered."

"*A Strange Kind of Love*. What about it?"

"Is it too late to change the dedication?"

"I'm afraid so. Why?"

"I'm not seeing that girl anymore."

Well, I went back to Yellow Springs and the academic year

finally ended, and in June I came back to New York and got a room at the Hotel Rio on West Forty-Seventh Street. I turned up at Scott Meredith one afternoon to pick up a check or drop off a manuscript, and I ran into a young fellow on a similar errand. It was Don, of course, who had quit editing and was freelancing, and who lived nearby himself, in a railroad flat on a very nasty block in the West Forties between Ninth and Tenth Avenues.

We introduced ourselves, and walked out of that office and into a friendship that lasted for fifty years. And that is why *A Girl Called Honey*, the first book in this triple volume and itself our initial collaborative effort, bears this dedication: "For Don Westlake and Larry Block, who introduced us."

I had one year to go at Antioch College, but it was not to be. Sometime that summer I got a letter from the school saying they'd come to the conclusion that I'd be happier elsewhere. And I knew they were right. I was already doing what I wanted to do, and I figured I'd keep on doing it.

But by the end of the summer I'd decided against doing it in New York, at least for the time being. I moved back to my parents' house in Buffalo, and I went on writing books for Bill Hamling of Nightstand Books and Harry Shorten and writing crime fiction for magazines. Don was doing much the same in New York. He and his wife and infant son were living in an awful block in Hell's Kitchen when we met and moved to the upper flat in a two-family house in Canarsie, Brooklyn, a ten minute walk from the Rockaway Parkway stop at the end of the Canarsie Line.

We stayed very much in touch. I don't think it ever occurred to either of us to pick up the phone; long-distance calls were for emergencies, or when somebody died. We wrote letters and probably put more creativity into that correspondence than into our work.

And somewhere along the way we discussed the possibility of collaborating. I wrote the first chapter of *A Girl Called Honey*. I sent a carbon copy to Don, and he wrote chapter two and sent it to me, and we continued in that vein until the book was done. We never discussed the plot or the characters. At one point I tired of a character he'd introduced and killed him off, whereupon Don retaliated by getting my character arrested for murder.

Damn, that was fun.

The lead's name was Honour Mercy Bane, and Don thought we should call the thing *Piece Without Honour*, and maybe we did. Who knows? We sent the manuscript to Henry, who sent it to Harry Shorten, who published it with the title it bears now. We split the money and decided we'd have to do it again sometime.

And did, before too long. The second book turned out to be *So Willing*, and Shorten published that one, too. I don't know what we called it, but it may have been *The Virgin Hunt*, or something like that. This time Don wrote the first chapter, and we tossed it back and forth until we had a book. I may have moved back to New York by then. Or not.

One of Don's chapters began, "Oh well, what the hell, there was always Adele." But when the book appeared some idiot at Midwood changed Adele's name to Della. God knows why. My best guess is that his mother's name was Adele, and he took umbrage.

If he were here, I'd tell him what he could do with his umbrage. And one of the first things that occurred to me when Bill Schafer proposed reprinting these books was that good old

Adele could have her name back. She wasn't even my character, it wasn't even my line, but I'll tell you, it's very satisfying to have it the way it was supposed to be.

The third book was *Sin Hellcat*, and it was brought out by our other mutual publisher, Bill Hamling at Nightstand Books. The first two books we wrote together were published "by Sheldon Lord and Alan Marshall," and that's the byline we tacked on *Hellcat*. But Hamling was having none of it. The book was published "by Andrew Shaw." I've no idea what our title may have been, but I'm sure it wasn't *Sin Hellcat*—not that there's anything wrong with it . . .

I blush to admit it, but I'm uncommonly proud of *Sin Hellcat*. If one writer had produced it, it would qualify as a tour de force; as the work of two pairs of hands, you could call it a tour de force majeure. As you'll see, it's a first-person narrative telling one story in sequential order, with other episodes of the narrator's prior life recounted one per chapter along the way.

What I like most about it is that it's no mean trick to tell which of us wrote a particular chapter. If I flip the book open and start reading, I can't necessarily tell myself. Somehow, without ever talking at all about the book during its writing, we matched our styles to a remarkable degree.

Oh, I could tell you now who wrote which chapters. But then I'd have to kill you.

Don and I never collaborated again after *Sin Hellcat*. Hal Dresner and I wrote a book called *Circle of Sinners* with a structure inspired by the film *La Ronde*: the viewpoint character in the first chapter has it off with someone, who becomes the viewpoint character in chapter two—and so on. Hamling published the book by either Andrew Shaw or Don Holliday, Hal's pen name. And I think we may have done a second book as well, but if so I can't recall anything about it.

Somewhere along the way, I collaborated with Bill Coons, a college friend of Don's who moved from Syracuse to New York to write Andrew Shaw novels. (He used my pen name and I vetted the books and took a cut.) At one point I started a book of my own, wrote three chapters, and hated it, so I took it around to Bill. "I can't stand what I've written here," I said, "so would you like to make it a collab? Write three chapters, and then we'll write alternate chapters until we have enough for a book, and we'll split what we get for it."

Bill agreed and tossed the manuscript on a table, and we went out for a drink. When he got home his wife had read the three chapters, the ones I said I couldn't stomach and assumed logically enough that Bill had written them. "I think you're really getting better," she told him. "This is far and away the best thing you've ever done."

Astonishing, isn't it, that the marriage didn't last?

Years later, Don collaborated with Brian Garfield on *Gangway!*, a comic western. That inspired Don's definition of collaboration as a process consisting of twice the work for half the money.

And then, years after that, some reader turned up at a signing and told me he thought Don and I should collaborate on a Bernie Rhodenbarr / John Dortmunder adventure. Readers are always making suggestions and I always hate them, but this one struck me as brilliant. Two professional criminals, both featured in lighthearted crime fiction—what could be a more natural combination?

But I could never get Don to go for it. At one point I wrote a first chapter, hoping it would get him into the spirit of things, but it didn't. He wasn't interested.

His initial objection was simple enough. The Bernie Rhodenbarr books were first person, the Dortmunder books third. A combination first- /third-person novel would read as if it had been designed by a Congressional committee.

I thought it would work just fine, but he wouldn't hear of it. A few years passed, and it struck me that nowhere was it carved in stone that Bernie had to narrate his stories. I could write about him in the third person.

Don allowed that might work, then, and he'd give it some real thought when he had finished his current projects. And he may have meant it, or he may have been polite, but in any case nothing ever came of it. I don't know that the world's any the poorer for the book we might have written, but I'll bet we'd have had fun with it.

As I write these lines, Don's been gone a year and a week. And our three joint novels are now available in this handsome hardcover edition. I'm happy about this, and I can only hope that Don would be pleased as well.

I can't be sure of that, as he hasn't had any say in the matter. I do know that, in recent years, he became increasingly open about pseudonymous work that he'd previously kept in the dark. Part of this may have stemmed from a recognition of the inevitability of it all. There are people out there practicing a weird form of scholarship on the crap we wrote—we, who thought of it so little. A quick Internet search can unearth no end of information about our early work, some of which may even be true. The genie, alas, is out of the bottle and the toothpaste is out of the tube. And, really, what difference does it make?

When Don agreed to have Hard Case Crime reissue some of his early books—crime novels, I should point out, that had nothing to apologize for—a mutual friend asked him why he thought this a good idea. The money didn't amount to much, after all, and the work was not as good as what he'd produced since then, and—

"The difference between being in print and out of print," Don told him, "is the same as the difference between being alive and being dead."

So I don't think it's too great an abuse of our friendship that I've shepherded these three books back into print, and am now sending them on their way into a new life as ebooks.

Books for Writers

THE LIAR'S BIBLE

In the fall of 1975 I spent a month on North Carolina's Outer Banks. Every day I fished off the Rodanthe pier, and every night I ate what I caught. It was a full life.

When I wasn't fishing, I sat in my room and wrote. Along with several short stories, I turned out an essay that attempted to answer the perennial (and perennially annoying) question of the non-writer to the writer: Where do you get your ideas? I discussed the way ideas crop up and how they turn into stories, and I mailed the piece off to *Writer's Digest* and forgot about it.

Six months later I remembered, when I learned that the magazine wanted to buy the article. I was in Los Angeles by then, living at the Magic Hotel, and my daughters would be flying out at the end of June to spend the summer with me. I figured they could keep me company at the hotel for July and we could spend August seeing something of the country on the way back to New York. And one of the places we'd stop en route would be Cincinnati, where *WD*'s editor, John Brady, could take me to lunch.

I had an agenda, and I shared it with him over bowls of the chili for which the city is famous. The magazine had several monthly columns, I pointed out, but what it didn't have was a column on the writing of fiction, and that seemed to be the chief interest of the greater portion of its subscribers. Surely they needed a fiction column, and surely I was the very person to write it.

Remarkably enough, Brady agreed with me. Maybe it was the chili. I wound up with an assignment to deliver 1,500 to 2,000 words every other month; they'd cut their cartoon columnist back to six issues a year, to alternate with *Fiction*.

I'd planned on returning to L.A. after I dropped off the kids, but wound up staying in New York. I rented a place on Bleecker Street and went to work. After I'd delivered three columns, Brady bumped the cartoon guy altogether and put me on a monthly schedule. I wrote that column, year in and year out, for fourteen years.

The piece that started it all, the essay I knocked out in Rodanthe when I wasn't hauling spot and croaker out of the Atlantic, wasn't the first I'd written about writing. Seventeen years earlier, in early 1958, I was a college student who'd dropped out to hang on to a summer job at a New York literary agency, quite the perfect learning experience for a wannabe writer. I spent eight hours a day reading fee scripts, the submissions of other wannabes who paid my boss to read their work. I was the one who read it, and it was my task to write letters over his signature detailing why their stories were unsalable, but assuring them that they were talented, and that they were best advised to write another story, and send it in. Uh, with another check, of course.

The moral and ethical aspects of all of this notwithstanding, it was a wonderful job. You learn more reading inept work than you could ever learn from a master. You see what's wrong. That's easier than trying to see what's right.

A couple of months into the job, I noticed one obvious error that a surprising number of my earnest hopefuls were committing. They used unwieldy verbs in dialogue, whipping out *Roget's Thesaurus* to avoid saying "said" all the time, and then wedding the verb to a cumbersome adverb. I wrote a piece about this, called it "Gloomily Asserted Smith," and gave it to Henry Morrison, who occupied the rung directly above mine on the Scott Meredith ladder. He sent it to a magazine called *Author and Journalist*, and, *mirabile dictu*, they bought it. I think they paid $25, but it might have been as much as $35; whatever it was, that's what I got . . . minus 10 percent for Scott, needless to say.

"Gloomily Asserted Smith" never led anywhere, unless you want to see it as a forerunner of my column. But the column itself led to four books.

The first, *Writing the Novel: From Plot to Print,* was the suggestion of Brady and his fellows in *WD*'s book division; by that time I'd been doing the column for a little over a year. It's been in print ever since.

The second and fourth were *Telling Lies for Fun and Profit* and *Spider, Spin Me a Web.* Both were composed of columns I'd written for the magazine, collected and arranged in some semblance of order. *Telling Lies* was published by Arbor House in hardcover and trade paperback, was a Book-of-the-Month Club alternate selection, and has been in print in one edition or another almost continuously since its 1981 publication.

Spider, Spin Me a Web was the same idea, but with columns written after those in *Telling Lies*. It came out from Writer's

Digest Books in 1988, and I've always felt it was the better book, but it's never sold nearly as well. The only obvious difference between the two books is the title, and if you think a title doesn't matter, well, you might want to rethink that one.

In 1983, I dreamed up an interactive seminar that would adapt some of the principles and techniques of the Human Potential Movement specifically for writers. I called it Write for Your Life, and for a couple of years my wife Lynne and I flew around the country with it. I realized there ought to be a book version and decided it was a natural for self-publishing, since I could sell it at seminars and promote it in the advertising for the seminar. And if I published it myself I could have copies right away, not a year later. In 1985 I printed 5,000 copies and sold them all; the book's available again, but in ebook form only.

In 1990 I came to a parting of the ways with the folks in Cincinnati. There was a change in the editorship, and the new boy felt a need to assert himself, and that was the end of my column. It was a shabby windup to fourteen good years, and it felt odd not to have a column due every month, but on balance I decided it was just as well. By then I'd long since exhausted everything I ever knew about writing. Time to hang it up and go on to other things.

So here, two decades later, is my fifth book on the subject. How on earth did that happen?

Well, it's not really all that hard to explain. *Telling Lies* gathered columns from my first four years at *WD*, *Spider* from the four or so years after that. That left a lot of columns uncollected, and in the ordinary course of things I would very likely have sorted through them and looked around for a publisher.

But when I rather abruptly stopped writing the column, I quit thinking about the subject. Lynne and I had just returned to New York after a couple of years in Florida and a couple more without a fixed address, and my career as a novelist was blossoming, which meant not only more books to write but more ancillary duties—book tours, promotional efforts, and the like.

Time passed. It'll do that.

And then, a couple of years ago, I heard from a fellow I know named Terry Zobeck. He's a fan and a collector, and his particular collecting interest is centered on the initial magazine appearance of works by those writers he most esteems. Toward this end he had compiled a great number of issues of *WD*, and by purchasing bulk lots he'd wound up with duplicate copies of many of those issues.

He'd checked them against his copies of my books, and established that he had a host of columns and articles of mine that had not appeared in either *Telling Lies* or *Spider.* That was more than enough uncollected material for a new book, and would he like me to send him his duplicate issues?

I could hardly say no. In addition to the duplicates, he went to the trouble of photocopying those columns of mine for which he had only a single copy. In all, I now had in hand 77 pieces that had never previously been published in book form, an ample amount for not one but two books.

So I thanked him profusely and put the box in the corner of my office and forgot about it for a couple of years.

Well, not exactly. I mean, I remembered just where it was, and sometimes I stared balefully at it. But I wasn't ready to do anything about it. I knew the material was worth publishing, but the whole process of getting it into shape for a traditional print publisher felt daunting, and I couldn't make myself believe that my own print publisher would be all that enthusiastic about it, or put forth much of an effort on its behalf.

Then Open Road came along, and set about publishing forty-plus backlist books of mine as ebooks. Whereupon one of those little lightbulbs took form over my head. (It was left over from the cartoon column, the one my own column displaced in *Writer's Digest*. See? Nothing's ever wasted.)

Print publication would have meant more work than I was prepared to undertake, and would have taken more time than I was willing to wait. And I don't know that the resultant book would have flown off shelves and out of stores. Publishing it as an Open Road E-Riginal has entailed hardly any work at all, and just look how little time it's required. I mean, here it is, right? Now that didn't take very long, did it?

If it's been wonderfully simple publishing this way, I've kept it every bit as simple so far as the volume's organization is concerned. In *Telling Lies* and *Spider*, I made an effort to group the columns by subject matter.

This time, I'm presenting everything in chronological order.

And I have to think that's not only the simplest and easiest way to do it, but the best as well. This way you'll be reading them in the order they were written. Which isn't to say that you can't skip around as the spirit moves you.

I am, as you may imagine, profoundly grateful to Terry Zobeck, but for whom this book would not exist. And I'm grateful as well to all my friends at Open Road, similarly indispensable; they made the book possible, and made my role in the process easy and pleasurable.

And I'm grateful to you, Dear Reader, as all of us who write can only be grateful to those who read our work. Isn't it remarkable, when one thinks of it, that the binary electronic blips and blops of e-publication can take something ephemeral by definition—words printed in magazines—and fix them in cyber-permanence?

Who knew?

THE LIAR'S COMPANION

For fourteen years, from 1976 to 1990, I wrote a column on the writing of fiction for *Writer's Digest*. At the very beginning it was an every-other-month affair, alternating with a column on cartooning, but in short order the magazine dropped the cartoonist, and my column went monthly.

I have to say it did me a world of good.

I make my living writing books, and it's an unstructured and uncertain occupation. So it did me good to have one specific thing to do every month, and to be assured of receiving a monthly check for it. The numbers on those checks were never enormous; I got $150 a column at the beginning, and coaxed enough raises out of them over the years to get that number up to $500 at the end. Now that was nothing to sneeze at, but neither was it anything to drool over.

But the money was the least of it.

Over the years, three books emerged. The first was *Writing the Novel from Plot to Print*, specifically commissioned by Writer's Digest Books after I'd been writing the column for a year or so. It's never been out of print, and now, I'm pleased to report, it's available as an Open Road ebook.

Next was *Telling Lies for Fun and Profit*. It was published in 1981, and composed of past columns, and I offered it to WD Books but the editor wasn't enthusiastic; my agent sent it to Don Fine at Arbor House, who published it in hardcover and trade paperback and placed it with the Book-of-the-Month Club.

WD Books looked at how *Telling Lies* was doing and felt they'd missed the boat, so when I had enough columns for a second volume, they got on board right away. I called the book *Spider, Spin Me a Web*. Both books have been in print pretty much continually since their original publication, and both are available now from HarperCollins in either trade paperback or ebook form.

That's been gratifying, believe me. When I write something, I really like to see it remain available for people to read. My great friend, the late Donald E. Westlake, was asked by a mutual friend why he'd agreed to the republication of some of his very early work. The money couldn't amount to that much, the friend said, so why bother with the deal?

"The difference between being in print and out of print," Don told him, "is the difference between being alive and being dead."

Right.

And yet the books aren't the most important benefit I got from that column, either.

I could string this out, and talk about other fringe benefits— that the column gave me sufficient credibility as a writer about writing so that I could successfully develop an interactional writing seminar and present it all over the country for a couple of years, that this in turn led to my writing and self-publishing a book version of the seminar. (*Write for Your Life*, and it too is available as a HarperCollins ebook.) That the column brought me speaking invitations. That it very likely led some people to have a look at my novels.

All true, and all good. But secondary, really, to the most important thing that column did for me, and I'll quit stalling now and tell you what that was.

It made me a better writer.

Once a month I had to come up with an idea for a column, some aspect of writing to address in around 1,800 words. Now after I'd been doing the column for a year or so, then-editor John Brady discovered flow charts, and decided that was what was needed for the optimal functioning of his editorial operation. So he wrote me a letter requesting that I supply him with the subjects I intended to cover in the next six months.

Now how the hell did I know? I didn't, obviously, and told him as much, and he told me this was really important, and after we'd gone back and forth a time or two more, I sat down and wrote out a list. Then, a month at a time, I wrote and submitted my columns, and not a one of them could be found on that list. So much for the flow chart.

I wasn't being deliberately contrary. (Well, maybe a little.) But there was no way I could know in advance what I'd be able to write about in a given month. There were more than a few months when I didn't know what I was going to write until the day when I sat down and wrote it.

But an idea always came along. I don't think I was ever once late with a column.

So it would seem that the need to produce a column was always very much in my mind, if not consciously on it. And one way or another this column-to-be-written informed both my reading and my writing.

It's a rare writer indeed who is not also a world-class reader. I had always been an omnivorous reader, and one blessed with a hearty appetite. When I became a writer, I immediately became a better reader; I found myself noticing what worked or didn't work in the story I was reading, and in turn became a better writer when I found myself applying what I'd noticed to my own work.

Writing about writing added another level to the whole enterprise. I continued to read for pleasure—I don't think I've ever been able to read in its absence—but now I would come across elements in what I read that got me thinking, and that now and then provided me with the subject matter for a future column.

Similarly, writing about writing made me more aware of elements in my own work.

I don't want to belabor this, it hardly seems worth it, so I'll just state it again and let it go at that: writing that column for fourteen years made me a better writer.

What on earth qualified me to tell people how to write?

I'd get that question occasionally, and it struck me as a reasonable one. I'd generally respond by explaining that I didn't tell people how to write, that I would never presume to do such a thing. While my column was instructional by definition, I didn't provide a lot of specific instruction. For the most part I talked about something I'd noticed in my work or another's, and how I'd solved (or at least coped with) something that had come up in the course of a book or story. I was endeavoring to share some of what I'd experienced and observed. If that constitutes teaching, then I was a teacher. If not, not.

Because I never thought of myself as teaching in the traditional sense, I never wanted to present the same lesson twice. *WD*'s various editors over the years would have liked to see me return to the same basic topics rather more often than I did. But I really wasn't interested in repeating myself.

Now in some magazines repetition is inevitable. If you've got a home gardening magazine, you can't decide not to write about tomatoes simply because you ran a comprehensive tomato article five years ago. There are folks out there who weren't reading the magazine back then, and the others, who've been with you all along, won't remember that old article. Or, even if they do, they won't mind reading it again.

But once I'd written something, I wouldn't go back to it unless I had something reasonably interesting to add. And that had its advantages, especially when it came time to collect the columns into a book. It wasn't just the same thing over and over again.

I stopped writing the column in 1990. It wasn't a very happy parting of the ways, and I left with a sour taste in my mouth. And I figured that all in all it was more than time for me to be done writing about writing. I seemed somehow to have written close to half a million words on the subject, and that was plenty.

And I had four books to show for it. That, too, was more than enough. Wasn't it?

Well, now there are six. A couple of months ago, Open Road brought out *The Liar's Bible: A Handbook for Fiction Writers*. And here we have *The Liar's Companion: A Field Guide for Fiction Writers*.

In a moment I'll tell you how they came to be, but first I want to say something about titles. My two books drawn from *WD* columns were *Telling Lies for Fun and Profit* and *Spider, Spin Me a Web*. I don't know that one is any better or stronger or more user-friendly than its fellow, but if I had to pick one over the other, I'd go with *Spider*. The columns are more recent, and I was very likely a little more knowledgeable when I wrote them.

Year in and year out, *Telling Lies* sells more copies than *Spider*. Like, *lots* more copies.

What's the difference? Well, obviously, the chief difference between the books lies in their titles. A great title, it's been often said, is a title on a bestselling book. *Telling Lies for Fun and Profit* is a great title.

Well, I'm no dummy. And that's why the two new books aren't called *The Spider's Bible* and *The Spider's Companion*.

But where did they come from?

Well, it's not really all that hard to explain. *Telling Lies* gathered columns from my first four years at *WD*, *Spider* from the four or so years after that. That left a lot of columns uncollected, and in the ordinary course of things I would very likely have sorted through them and looked around for a publisher.

But when I rather abruptly stopped writing the column, I quit thinking about the subject.

And then, a couple of years ago, I heard from a fellow I know named Terry Zobeck. He's a fan and a collector, and his particular collecting interest is centered on the initial magazine appearance of works by those writers he most esteems. Toward this end he had compiled a great number of issues of *WD*, and by purchasing bulk lots he'd wound up with duplicate copies of many of those issues.

He'd checked them against his copies of my books, and established that he had a host of columns and articles of mine that had not appeared in either *Telling Lies* or *Spider*. That was more than enough uncollected material for a new book, and would he like me to send him his duplicate issues?

I could hardly say no. In addition to the duplicates, he went to the trouble of photocopying those columns of mine for which he had only a single copy. In all, I now had in hand 77 pieces that had never previously been published in book form, an ample amount for not one but two books.

So I thanked him profusely and put the box in the corner of my office and forgot about it for a couple of years. Making use of the material promised to be a whole lot of work, and I wasn't sure a print publisher would be that enthusiastic anyway.

Then Open Road came along, and set about publishing forty-plus backlist books of mine as ebooks. I'd long since come to believe that ebooks are the future of publishing, and it's beginning to look as though the future has arrived, and not a moment too soon. I asked the Open Road folks if they'd be interested in a pair of books on the gentle art of prevarication, and they responded with great enthusiasm, and we were on our way.

So now I'm the author of six instructional books for writers. And no, I don't think writing can be taught, but I know it can be learned. Most of us learn in two ways, by reading and by writing. (I found a third way to add to the mix: by writing *about* writing.) What we read and what we write, and the extent to which we'll find it helpful, is very much an individual matter. Some people say they've found what I've written about writing to be useful reading matter. I hope that turns out to be true for you.

Sometimes I'm asked what's the one piece of writing advice I consider most important.

Write to please yourself, I reply.

That's not all there is to it, not by any means. But there's nothing without it.

* * *

WRITING THE NOVEL: FROM PLOT TO PRINT

In the spring of 1976 I sold a piece to *Writer's Digest*, the monthly magazine for writers. I was in Los Angeles at the time, in mute testimony to H. L. Mencken's observation that a Divine Hand had taken hold of the United States by the State of Maine, and lifted, whereupon everything loose wound up in Southern California. The article I sold them was a reply to the perennial question, *Where do you get your ideas?*, and when they accepted it I got an idea on the spot.

My idea was to sell them on the idea of hiring me as a columnist. They had a couple of columnists, but nobody was writing about fiction, and that was the chief interest of most of their audience, so the need seemed to be there. Rather than push this through the mail, I waited until I could do it in person; my daughters flew out in July to spend the summer with me, and we stayed that month in L.A. and spent the month of August on a leisurely drive back to New York, where they lived with their mother—and where I had lived, until that Divine Hand sent me spinning.

I mapped out our route east so that I could work in a lunch in Cincinnati with John Brady, then the editor at *Writer's Digest*. He'd bought my article, and over lunch he bought my idea for a fiction column, to run six times a year, alternating with their cartoon column. I got back to New York and sent in the first column, and by the time I'd written the third one they'd booted the cartoonist. My column would appear in the magazine every month for the next fourteen years.

I'd been doing it for a little over a year when Brady got in touch. Their book division felt the need for a book telling how to write a novel. And they liked the way I wrote about writing, and wanted me to do the book for them.

I was living in New York again, in an apartment on Greenwich Street. (It's no more than a two-minute walk from where I live now, thirty-three years later, but I've had a slew of addresses in the interim.) I wrote the book and sent it off, and the folks in Cincinnati liked it just fine, and proposed a title: *Writing the Novel from Plot to Print.*

I didn't like it at the time, felt it made the whole process sound more mechanical than I thought it to be. I'd made a particular point in my book of not telling the reader, "This is the way to do it." There were, as I saw it, at least as many ways to do it as there were writers, and arguably as many ways as there were books. But they really liked the title, and I went along with it, and I have to say it seems OK to me now.

The book has remained continually in print for more than thirty years. I guess the title hasn't hurt it any.

Fifteen years ago, Writer's Digest Books wanted me to revise *Writing the Novel.* They felt it was dated. I talk about the Gothic novel, for example, and while books fitting that pattern may continue to be written and read, the category by that name has long since ceased to exist. If I could go through it and update it, then they could bring out a new edition with the words "updated new edition" on it, and increase sales accordingly.

I thought about it, and ultimately decided against it. The book seemed to be one readers find useful, and the techniques and principles discussed struck me as essentially timeless, as pertinent in 1995 as they had been in 1978. And the whole idea of updating a book bothers me, anyway. I knew a writer once who'd updated a novel, or tried to; it was being reissued after fifteen or twenty years, and he'd gone through it page by page, updating the cost of a telephone call from a nickel to a dime (this was a few years ago), changing the stars of a movie his character watches from William Powell and Myrna Loy to William Holden and June Havoc (yes, this was a while ago), and otherwise altering the book's temporal setting.

Well, it didn't work. One way or another, every word in that book was attached to the year it was written. It had a certain integrity, and you altered it at your peril.

Writing the Novel is not a novel, and thus may not need to adhere to the same standard of artistic integrity, but it's nonetheless a creature of the time of its writing, and my inclination is to leave it alone. I'm also predisposed to avoid work, and this looked to me to be work to no purpose.

Now, fifteen years after I decided the book wasn't broke and didn't need to be fixed, it is in fact another decade and a half older, and that much further out of date. But it still ain't broke, as I can tell by the enthusiastic word-of-blog I keep encountering on the Internet, and I'm still predisposed to avoid work. So I'm not fixing it. I hope it does for you all a book of this sort can possibly hope to do. I hope it helps you speak in your own voice, map out your own route, and find your very own way to your very own book.

Bon voyage!

Afterword

How can a book like *Afterthoughts* not have an afterword? I don't think I need to follow the precepts of the legendary preacher though: "First I tell 'em what I'm about to tell 'em, then I tell 'em, and then I tell 'em what I just told 'em." So instead I'll give you a chance to tell me whatever you want.

Contact information for Lawrence Block:
Website: www.lawrenceblock.com
Email: lawbloc@gmail.com
Twitter: @LawrenceBlock
Facebook: www.facebook.com/lawrence.block

If you like this book, I hope you'll let me know.

And if you like it a whole lot, I hope you'll let *everybody* know!

Thanks!

Cover design by Jason Gabbert
Interior design by Andrea C. Uva

ISBN 978-1-4532-3934-6

Published in 2011 by Open Road Integrated Media
180 Varick Street
New York, NY 10014
www.openroadmedia.com

EBOOKS BY LAWRENCE BLOCK

FROM OPEN ROAD MEDIA

 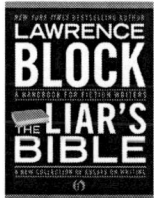 

  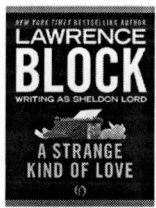

Available wherever ebooks are sold

OPEN ROAD

INTEGRATED MEDIA

Videos, Archival Documents, and New Releases

Sign up for the Open Road Media newsletter and get news delivered straight to your inbox.

FOLLOW US:
@openroadmedia and
Facebook.com/OpenRoadMedia

CPSIA information can be obtained at www.ICGtesting.com
Printed in the USA
LVOW120409040112

262291LV00001B/108/P